LEARNING TO
TRUST
THE FATHER'S HEART

FOREWORD BY TIM HILL

LEARNING TO
TRUST
THE FATHER'S
HEART

CHRISTAL BAILEY

HGR Editorial Services
Homer G. Rhea, Managing Editor
Cecily Rhea, Editor
Nellie Keasling, Copy Editor
Lonna Gattenby, Layout and Cover Design
Homer8238@gmail.com

ISBN: 978-1-64288-211-7

Published by Pathway Press
Cleveland, TN 37311
Printed in the United States of America

Truly Yours

A dad will teach you how to fly and let you keep the wings.
He'll build a stage and mix the sound, but you're the one who sings.

He'll show you how to hold a brush and stretch the canvas on its frame.
Then guide uncertain fingers 'til paint and painted are the same.
And when the work of art is done, its artist to proclaim,
The sole inscription to be found is where he wrote your name.

If ever you should wonder if these arts are yours to ply,
Know they were only his to give you; they're yours to multiply.
And in the eons yet to come, like stars across the midnight sky,
The light of you and yours and theirs means he may never die.

A dad will teach you how to fly and let you keep the wings.
He'll build a stage and mix the sound, but you're the one who sings.

—Christal, Farah, and Aaron's Dad

Dedication

To My Daddy,

You have faithfully demonstrated the love of the
heavenly Father to our family,
and I am forever grateful!

I love you!

Table of Contents

FOREWORD

Almost no one can dispute the meaning or the importance of the word *trust*. It is a very "cut-and-dried" concept, leaving little room for misinterpretation; you either trust something—or someone—or you don't. Once a trust is violated, there can be demonstrations of a turnaround, but ultimately, it becomes extremely difficult to place complete trust back into a situation or person who has at one time betrayed a trust.

Numerous references can be found to the word *trust* in the Bible. Perhaps the most quoted is "Trust in the Lord with all your heart, and lean not on your own understanding (Proverbs 3:5 NKJV). Psalm 56:3 says, "When I am afraid, I put my trust in you" (NIV). Other passages in Psalms include, "Commit your way to the Lord; trust in him and he will do this" (37:5 NIV), and, "Blessed is the one who trusts in the Lord, who does not look to the proud" (40:4 NIV). And Jeremiah 17:7 says, "But blessed is the one who trusts in the Lord, whose confidence is in him" (NIV).

Trust can be equated to faith. Both require a level of belief and discipline to be effective in a believer's life. Both represent a willingness to place one's life in God's hands and "trust" the outcome. While it may sound easy, abandoning worry and apprehension goes against every natural human instinct. As much as we would love to be able to release everything by placing it into His hands, we inevitably hold back at least a portion, raising our levels of stress and anxiety. To truly reach a level of complete trust is a rare gift.

Every believer has a journey in this realm of trust. Heeding the call by God to do so, Christal Bailey tells her story and addresses the process of releasing our burdens to a loving God in whom we can place complete trust. Through a lifetime of prayer and ministry, Christal speaks with a voice of experience and godly authority. Finding the right path in trusting God's will and direction is a rewarding and life-changing endeavor that Christ-followers should all strive to accomplish. *Learning to Trust the Father's Heart* can be a valuable resource in reaching that level of trust.

—Tim Hill
General Overseer
Church of God, Cleveland, Tennessee

ACKNOWLEDGMENTS

The following people have played a supporting role in this book's coming into fruition:

- My precious family who has helped make many of the memories told in this book. I say a special "Thank you"!
- My husband, Rob, for whom I am more than grateful for his support, love, and many hours spent listening to my ideas and reading over my stories. I could not have done this without you!
- My son, Tobie, who is a wonderful writer and always encouraged me by saying, "Just be yourself, mom, and write from your heart."
- My mom who continually reinforces, in one way or another: "All things are possible, for those who believe."
- Farah and Aaron, thank you for helping me recall childhood accounts and cheering me on.

Introduction

As for God, His way is perfect;
the word of the Lord is proven;
He is a shield to all who trust in Him
(Psalm 18:30).

A year after the Father lovingly instructed me to write (and a year after I had defiantly dragged my feet), I sat in a women's conference in Tampa, Florida. Women were all around me; yet I felt He had a spotlight on me, and I would not be able to escape our much-needed conversation. Once again, I heard His loving voice, but this time His petition was different. I sensed this would be His last pull at my heart, and I would be left with a great sense of regret if I decided not to yield. My list of reasons why I could not write did not matter, and my cop-outs were now a moot point. I had grumbled my objections and feelings of inferiority for long enough, and I knew that if I dismissed His guidance, I would find myself in a place of remorse. Not merely because of a missed opportunity, but also because my act of obedience would pivot my relationship with Him forward. For these and a myriad of unmentioned reasons, I knew that I could no longer shy away from this assignment.

During a season of fasting, I sat at the kitchen counter, ready to begin this endeavor. But a blank screen mockingly glared back at me. *What now?* I thought as I stared back at my computer. I took a deep breath and prayed, "Lord, I am clueless what to do now. Please speak to me." Instantly He reminded me, "Every new home, new ministry, new endeavor you have anointed and dedicated to Me. Why is this any different?" I grabbed the olive oil out of the kitchen cabinet, applied a thin layer to my hands, and swiped it across my keyboard.

"Father, this one is Yours.
Yours only to be set apart for Your purposes."

As some say, an immediate "download" from heaven transpired, as He began telling me what the book would be about and giving me stories to share. Knowing then that I would be writing about trust and the correlation between my earthly father and my heavenly Father, ideas flowed. Feeling nostalgic, I wrote several stories, showing the parallels of the two, and the lessons I learned.

Despite all His encouragement and confirmations, I kept silent concerning His instructions. Not even my husband was brought into the loop, knowing if I shared, my safety net would be removed and the probability of backing out less likely. I needed more reassurance and waited to go much further.

Six months passed, writing a little here, a little there, but nothing much to speak of. Downplaying the assignment helped the unnerving angst I had self-imposed. Needing a breakthrough, I asked the Father for one more stamp of approval before beginning, "I know what you have asked, Lord, but I'm requesting one more confirmation. Please allow someone to give me just one word, *trust*. That's all. Just one word."

Learning to Trust the Father's Heart

Only a few weeks later, I stood at an altar in New York City praying with those who had responded to my husband's appeal, when Pastor Sante approached. With a sweet smile on his face, he said, "The Lord told me to tell you that you had asked for one word—the word, my sister, is *trust*. That's all you need; so, just trust Him."

"Thank You, Jesus!" was all I could say.

Afterward, Rob asked me, "What was that all about?"

I replied, "There's a lot to this, but I will fill you in later."

My head was still swimming with wonder and amazement at my Father's confirmation. Rob smiled and said, "Was it regarding the book the Lord said you are to write?" I had not told him yet! But the Lord had, and in doing so, completely removed whatever safety net of escape I thought I still had. The Lord had revealed our secret, and now I would have to be all in. So, I did not start this journey with perfect trust or complete confidence, but rather day-by-day obedience. Throughout this process, walls of fear have crumbled as I have felt His nearness and have had peace in the knowledge that I have not been alone in the process.

I hope that some of the snapshots of my life story, combined with nuggets from the Word of God, will birth reliance and faith in the Father in those who read this book. And may your faith and trust in Him grow as you willingly and fully surrender to His plan for your life! As I've written, my memories took me back to simpler times in my life where my earthly father demonstrated the love and trustworthiness of my heavenly Father. This childlike faith and trust is the home in which our Father longs for His people to reside.

Without trust, living a life of unbelief is far too normal. Relationships without trust are bombarded with questions looming over every encounter, monitoring every move to make sure they follow through on their word. People can

1
Trust While You Wait

Trust in the LORD *with all your heart,*
and lean not on your own understanding
(Proverbs 3:5 MEV).

For the first five years of my life, I sat on my dad's lap every night for dinner. Listening to my parents discuss their day and lay out the groundwork for the next day made me feel included. On Friday nights, it was always a challenge for me to sit still during mealtime because of my excitement for the next day. As I sat there trying my best to behave and finish my meal, I would overhear my parents talking and making their plans. Knowing Saturdays would be spent with my favorite person, the excitement was more than I could contain! I'm sure that the entirety of their to-do list was a chore for them, but, to my imagination, it was an adventure waiting.

After dinner, you would find the two of us sitting in his large, golden armchair, with his favorite TV snack, a bowl of pepperoncini peppers, watching either boxing, *M.A.S.H*, *Hogan's Heroes*, or *All in the Family* reruns together. Drawing in my knees and curling up under his arm like a dachshund trying to burrow under a blanket, I felt warm and safe. I listened to his heartbeat and never wanted to leave that comfortable, safe place. I was hidden from the world and had high hopes that Mom would never find me and enforce bath and bedtime. Nonetheless, time swiftly passed, and my mom would stand over me. I whimpered my objections, but with Dad's stern look and kiss on the forehead, I headed to bed. Escalating anticipation made it challenging to fall asleep, but I knew that was the ideal way to make the time pass.

Waking up the next morning to the smell of coffee, sausage, and bacon, I leaped out of bed and raced down the hallway. It just felt right to see Bugs Bunny and Road Runner shows playing on the television and Mom scurrying around the house. Here we go . . . the best day of the week was underway.

On Saturdays, my dad occupied himself with work at home and made it a point to include me. Regular mundane tasks became thrilling on these action-packed days, as I worked and learned. Dad was busy in the kitchen, wearing his favorite cut-off jean shorts and making breakfast. He handed me the whisk to stir the gravy while he scrambled eggs, all the while telling one of his classic stories. Before we knew it, breakfast was over, and we were on to our busy day. This day, not unlike the rest, was filled with yard work, car repairs, shoeing horses, fixing everything in the house I had broken that past week, and Mom's honey-do list.

WOOD CHIPS FLYING

The word *lazy* and Stephen McCarter have never been used in the same sentence, so working with him was always full of adventure and excitement. Dad is a jack-of-all-trades and an excellent teacher. There is nothing he cannot build, fix, or create, and I was inevitably stuck to his side, soaking in every possibility. Instead of being annoyed by my presence, he always wanted and included me, enjoying our time together.

One of Dad's specialties is storytelling. His ability to articulate emotions and shape words into images that one can see and almost feel is impressive. I've always loved hearing his stories, and he has never been in short supply! One story that he told is about one of our Saturdays when I was an enthusiastic preschooler, ready to embrace every possibility that came my way.

One brisk Saturday morning in 1978, Dad was chopping wood, and I refused to stay far enough away to be safe. As he swung his ax, wood chips were flying. He gave me clear instructions to, "Stay back," but I continued to creep closer and closer. After all, I was more than capable of helping. Stopping multiple times to move me away from the danger, he realized his straightforward approach wasn't getting him very far. Expecting me to understand his reasoning was clearly not working. Despite his direct and emphatic directions that I was not supposed to get close, the urge to help him was overwhelming. He knew he needed another plan. "Baby, I need you to help me out with an important job." He had my full and undivided attention. While pointing to a tree several yards away, he continued, "I need you to hold on to that tree and do not let go."

I am sure I wholeheartedly believed he needed my assistance, so I was all-in! He continued, "It is extremely important to me that you hold on to that limb and do not move." Patiently, he waited while I tried to get this perfect. "No, no, no, not that tree, the limb on the other tree." Without squawking at me or becoming frazzled, he gently guided my path to his intended location. "Good job, baby, now hold it tight and don't let go. Hold it for me." I was helping him work; I was a part of his plan. That being the case, I was content to hold on to that tree for as long as he needed.

I may not have understood why I was holding that tree, or that my father's intention was to keep me safe, but my dad needed me to hold it, so I held it.

WHERE DID YOU DETOUR?

Learning to hold on, trust, and let the Father do His job can, at times, cause us frustration, anxiety, and fear—none of which come from the Lord. More times than not, we feel we must have more of a say, more control, more contribution, give more advice, and consequently we inch closer and closer to the danger. Wood chips are flying, axes are swinging, and we are dodging in and out of chaos.

> **"***Learning to hold on, trust, and let the Father do His job can, at times, cause us frustration, anxiety, and fear— none of which come from the Lord.* **"**

Trust, I believe, is the vital missing link for many, and a lack of trust ultimately hinders us from living in the promises of God. If we are willing to be transparent and to honestly evaluate our lives and the situations in which we find ourselves involved, the Lord will begin revealing the path that led us to our current destination. The road map with which we have navigated our lives, more times than not, has an exit where we detoured off course and allowed doubt and disbelief to appear. Trust disappeared, and we are not even sure how we arrived where we are currently residing.

A question I often ask is, how can we have childlike faith and the dependence we once had with our earthly father, with our heavenly Father? How do we simply hold on and allow Him to protect us while He works? Can we trust His care and guidance while the unsettling chips of life begin flying? Will we hold on to the tree and trust our Father, or choose to lean on our own understanding? If we are honest, we know our understanding compared to His is downright laughable, and yet time after time, we defer to it.

We make decisions based on our ability to see and understand, knowing we cannot see the full span of our life or know how one piece completes the next. Yes, we play a significant part in this journey, but it is not as important as we may sometimes think. We know we need Him, but we feel as though we should have the lead role. However, if we are going to live a life that is in complete solidarity with the Father, we must submit the leading role to Him. We must be willing to trust Him enough to abdicate our position as the leader of our lives and defer everything to Him.

> **" *We must be willing to trust Him enough to abdicate our position as the leader of our lives and defer everything to Him.* "**

As my dad tells the story, I happily held the tree for well over a preschooler's attention span. What would have seemed like a lifetime passed by quickly as I engaged in my very active imagination. Shaking me back into reality, he shouted, "Good job, baby girl, you can let go." Proud of the job we had accomplished, hand in hand we moved on to what was next on our checklist. As I grew older, his trust in me grew, and I was allowed more and more responsibility.

Our heavenly Father has the same plan for us as well. He wants us to trust Him, to allow His hand to guide us, and to grow! When we fully understand who is in control and why, we yield to His high authority.

TEACHABLE MOMENTS

My dad's story of trust and obedience portrays a sweet little girl who was happy to comply with her father's wishes. This was not the typical story of my childhood. Most lessons learned did not come with quiet compliance, a submissive will, or without failure. I needed to understand the whys and why nots. I felt it necessary to have a complete understanding, but for most circumstances questioning those in authority was unacceptable. "Yes, Sir," as you can imagine, would be the best choice of words. However, for my inquisitive mind, that was a struggle.

Snippets of my childhood were like, "Don't touch the box-cutter, baby, that could really hurt you." Two minutes later, he was tightly holding my sliced open thumb under the kitchen sink and saying, "Don't look." Which of course I did; I had to look. Traumatized by the sight of blood, uncontrollable screams followed. There were countless lessons that I insisted on learning the hard way. There were experiences that never had to happen, if only I had trusted that he had my best interests at heart and had not allowed my curiosity to take over.

Even as a young child, I primarily leaned on my own understanding. Sure, I trusted my father, but not to the point I was willing to altogether resign my will to his. As a good father, he wanted me to have input, be stretched, have opinions, and grow into the woman I was created to be. He had more life experience, so he was fully aware that growing was a process that took time. He understood the importance of unwavering patience during this venture of parenthood. Thankfully, my dad, for the most part, was patient and had a knack for finding extremely creative ways of teaching and punishing.

He took advantage of every opportunity to speak into the lives of his children, and discipline was no exception. His punishments were just as creative as he was and never failed to be full of teachable moments. Of course, my siblings and I had the regular spankings and groundings from time to time, but Dad hated those. I think they were too ordinary for him. He was more inclined to make us write papers, dig holes, get out of bed three hours early, or any memorable way to make an impression.

I lived in the same home for almost eighteen years, and, most of that time, the five of us shared one bathroom. For some illogical reason, I never could remember to put the toothpaste lid back on the tube after brushing my teeth. This drove my dad crazy, and after several warnings, the punishment was handed down. I was to unscrew the toothpaste lid, lay it on the counter, raise up both hands, pick up the lid again, and completely tighten the cap back on the tube. This exercise was supposed to continue for thirty minutes. Insistent that I follow these instructions to the tee, he watched as I reluctantly and begrudgingly worked. Approximately ten minutes into the punishment, after a blister began to develop on my thumb, he gave mercy and allowed me to stop. To this day, you will always find my toothpaste of choice has a flip-top lid. Memory made, and lesson learned!

As an adult, I have complete trust in my dad. I would blindly follow him anywhere, because he has proven, many times over, his faithfulness to me. I wholeheartedly trust his decisions, life experience, and more important, his love for me. He would never stray, never even consider offering poor advice, and always weigh out what is best for my life. However, that level of trust and reliance develops over time. Proven, tried, and true, it is an authentic demonstration of love.

THE LIST

As I held that tree, I waited without a care in the world; I blissfully daydreamed while Dad finished the job. Even then, I had the mental wherewithal to rest, even for a few moments, in the fact that he knew what he was doing, and I was content in being part of his big plan. I was developing a trust that would unequivocally stand the test of time. My primary task was to give him control and trust him to do what he knew best.

Waiting can be difficult. Planning ahead and having an agenda brings peace and comfort to my life. Without a plan, I can fall into an anxious place, which leads to questioning and doubt. I find myself inundated with thoughts of what's next and what's the best way to accomplish "the list." My husband inherently is aware when my mind is reeling, and with a knowing smile brings to my attention, "You're doing it again . . . checking off the list in your head." He knows because that's precisely what is happening. Every time I say, "Okay" out loud, it's a checkmark on my list. Also, with each "Okay," I am releasing a little of the self-imposed pressure with which I naturally wrap myself.

When I step back and take a hard look at how I operate, I realize the comfort I feel is not entirely connected to the plan or "the list." The truth is that my comfort comes from being in control. God operates best when He holds the reigns, but I sometimes find it difficult to relinquish my grip. I want to orchestrate the journey and the outcome. If asked, I would argue the fact that I trust Him with my whole heart. Convincing myself of this fact, the Father whispers, "This isn't how trust looks. It is how control looks."

>   " *Our fractured emotions tend to get in the way of the bravery needed to trust completely.* "

So how do you trust while you wait? When you feel helpless? When turbulence is surrounding at all times, and you are only allowed to stay put and weather the storm? It is a test of will to fully trust God when circumstances are swirling, and you have no sway, influence, or say in the matter. Our fractured emotions tend to get in the way of the bravery needed to trust completely.

As my dad did, God gives explicit instructions for us to back up and let Him work. Instead, we inch closer and closer to the danger because we are convinced we can help. Maybe the truth is hidden behind our desire, not to be helpful, but to be in control. We have such resistance in relying implicitly on Him that we deplete every ounce of energy we have to persuade Him to do it our way. One-sided negotiations begin. While He is chipping away and working on our behalf, we continually interrupt His work because we need reassurance. How many times have I been guilty, and how many times has He been patient? How do we trust and be content holding that tree while He does what only He can do?

POSTPONING THE ANNOUNCEMENT

In Luke, we read about the life of the priest Zechariah and his wife Elizabeth. They served God faithfully and obeyed His commands. Luke 1:5-7 says,

> When Herod was king of Judea, there was a priest by the name of Zechariah from the priestly group of Abijah. His wife Elizabeth was from the family of Aaron. Both of them were good people and pleased the Lord God by obeying all that he had commanded. But they did not have children. Elizabeth could not have any, and both Zechariah and Elizabeth were already old (CEV).

They had become accustomed to waiting for their prayers to be answered. They had asked God for a child. They knew He was able to give them their miracle; however, He waited. Now late in life, long after hope was lost, they were given a promise by God in verses 13-14, "But the angel told him: Don't be afraid, Zechariah! God has heard your prayers. Your wife Elizabeth will have a son, and you must name him John. His birth will make you very happy, and many people will be glad" (CEV).

With her lifelong prayer answered, she still postponed sharing this life-changing news. Luke 1:24 says she waited five months to share with others about her pregnancy. Why was she waiting? I wonder if, at this point, she had accepted her barrenness and no longer dreamed of life growing in her womb. Had all the waiting given her permission to forfeit trust? Maybe she had allowed her hopes to rise in the past, only to discover she was not expecting. Perhaps she had been vulnerable, sharing the news only to suffer the anguish of a miscarriage. I wonder how many times she thought this time would be different, "God is answering my longings," only to have her hope crushed with heart-break. Did her trust in God crumble a little each time the answer was no?

I think about her husband during this time. Did he try to share with her what the angel had told him? He had experienced an encounter with the heavenly, and she had not. Zechariah had the privilege of seeing and speaking to an angel, and she had not. What reassurance that must have given him, but did he find a way to share this with Elizabeth?

I love the angel's powerful words in verse 20, "Everything will take place when it's supposed to" (CEV). Zechariah struggled to believe the word of the Lord, and possibly because he and Elizabeth had believed before and had been disappointed. Although this time, it was so blatantly visible. An angel spoke it to ensure the clarity of the message. The word was more than his heart could believe. Punishment for his doubt was handed down, and for more than nine months, he could not speak. Nevertheless, it wasn't too late for him. Another chance was given to declare the Lord's plan, and Zechariah boldly disclosed the child's name would not be what others expected. He would see and actively be involved with the promise despite his questioning. The destiny of the revelation could not be stopped! Sure, his life changed for a season because of the Lord's correction, but it was not too late. His doubt and distrust would not be allowed to dictate the outcome.

THE SECRET IS OUT

How often have we been able to relate to Zechariah? Knowing without a doubt isn't the question. We heard the Lord and understood what He declared over our lives. We know it was His voice. Then how can we see with clarity the revelation and turn the other direction? How can we possibly know beyond a shadow of a doubt what God is revealing and still disregard His voice? And yet, just as Zechariah did, we do. We buy into the belief that if we ignore it, it will go away. Ignorance is bliss, right? Wrong. We are convincing ourselves to disregard the promise and bury the vision.

Like any other death, you bury and you grieve. When God gives you a revelation that you blatantly disregard, you ultimately bury part of yourself. Missed opportunities bombard your mind with, "What if" and "if only." We find ourselves spiraling into a downward dimension of regrets and grief; the enemy kicks into full gear, jumping on our backs, pushing us deeper into the darkness.

 When God gives you a revelation that you blatantly disregard, you ultimately bury part of yourself.

Although the revelation was clearly visible, that shred of doubt gave you permission to overthink and dismiss instructions given by the Lord. Thankfully, all it takes is one cry, and the Father pulls you out of the darkness. A sliver of hope from Him will far outweigh the shred of doubt from the enemy. Learn, dust yourself off, get your bearings, and start again. Choose His voice and determine in your heart to trust and believe. Next time will be different. As He did for Zechariah, He will forgive and restore your voice, too.

Luke 1:23-25 reads:

> So it was, as soon as the days of his service were completed, that he departed to his own house. Now after those days his wife Elizabeth con-

ceived; and she hid herself five months, saying, "Thus the Lord has dealt with me, in the days when He looked on *me*, to take away my reproach among people."

Elizabeth reached a point where she couldn't hide any longer. There was no turning back. The secret was out, so no more playing it safe. She had to take the risk. Her promise was on the way, and whatever was holding her back was no longer an issue worth pondering. The child, the promise, was all that mattered. Fear, anxiety, and disbelief had no place. The baby was saying, "Ready or not, here I come." The promises we are hiding, keeping safe, afraid to believe in are saying, "Ready or not here we come." If you think about the journey of raising children, natural or spiritual, that's how it goes. We keep them safe and protected. We spend our days baby-proofing, feeding, training, teaching, nurturing until our child is ready to go on their own and say, "I've had enough milk. I'm tired of holding back. I want to show the world what I am made of." With what feels like throwing caution to the wind, they let go, and, in turn, we let go.

Zechariah and Elizabeth had a gift that God had prepared for them from day one. The timing was critical not only for them but for the Savior of the world. Their miracle had to come into alignment with the appointed time for the Messiah. God knew what was coming for them, and He heard every prayer, but His answer was to wait. *Wait* is not a word I'm very fond of; however, there is purpose in the waiting. Trusting God while you wait on the promise you are to receive does not make the process pleasurable. God anxiously waits for the time to come when He can say, "You are ready. Here's the gift I have for you. Now, you can let go!"

HIS INDESCRIBABLE GIFT

Our daughter, Victoria, always tells us when she buys a gift, and she can't wait to tell us all about it. She can't control herself. "Hey, Mom," . . . and precedes to tell me detail after detail until she has given away the surprise. Usually, a picture follows the call or text stream. She loves gift-giving and cannot wait to share. How much more does the Father want to provide us with the gifts He has for us. Gifts that are just waiting for us. Matthew 7:11 says, "If you, then, though you are evil, know how to give good gifts to your children, how much more will your Father in heaven give good gifts to those who ask him!" (NIV).

God is ready and willing to give treasured gifts to His children and longs for us to reach out and ask. The questions to ponder, if you are willing or inclined, are: *Will you wait for the answer? Will you choose to accept His indescribable gift in the time frame He sees fit?* The truth is whether we hold on and trust, or fight, kicking and screaming the entire way. Everything will take place when it's supposed to, just as the angel said.

Trust waits . . . not in a delayed response, but waiting for His voice, instructions, and guidance. He's a God who moves into action for those who wait for Him. Don't jump ahead of His plans or try to orchestrate the details. Listen to what David says, "Wait on the LORD; Be of good courage, and He shall strengthen your heart; Wait, I say, on the LORD!" (Psalm 27:14).

Waiting is not wasting time, but rather, waiting is working. It is working out the spiritual details, adjusting character, strengthening weak spots in the armor, aligning destinies, filling in the gaps, and arranging the perfect timing. Never is a second wasted with the Lord. He is strengthening your heart, catapulting you into realms of greatness you have not dared to believe. Emboldened by your trust in Him, you move forward, conquering the adventure He has laid out for your life. Every detail of His checklist can and *will* come to fruition. To your Father, the importance of your life's calling is of monumental significance.

Trusting Him is the primary objective. Hold on to the tree, instead of caving to the pressures of life, allowing childlike dependence to take over. Choose daily to trust His ways, even when understanding is beyond you, and remain content in His big plan. He is waiting for you to call on His name. He is leaning in and listening for His child to cry, "Father!"

2
Trust His Name

Some trust in chariots and some in horses, but we trust in the name of the LORD our God
(Psalm 20:7 NIV).

Over a few years, everything I had grown accustomed to changed. Our family began to grow. First, my little sister was born, and then it wasn't long before our little brother followed. As time passed even further, it seemed odd to hear my mom calling my two siblings to our dinner table. One of the worst of the injustices was having to share my dad's lap! As I battled the jealousy and tried my best to process my feelings, I needed reassurance of my place among these new dynamics. Most of my fears and anxieties were unfounded and having a younger sister and a younger brother turned out okay. My new normal turned out to be fun, especially on the weekends. On these wonderful Saturday mornings, our dad would call out, "Christal, Farah, Aaron, let's go!" And off we would go into a Steve McCarter adventure.

One particular Saturday when I was nine years old, Dad had prepared a surprise for us. Mom's task was to keep us inside until he was ready for the big reveal! So, there we were, bunched up as close to the door as we could be, waiting as patiently as this wild crew possibly could. We were so eager to see what was on the other side of that door and find out what mystery awaited us. I did my best to help Mom keep my four- and two-year-old siblings at bay, but we were more than ready for the door to be opened and to be set free into the great outdoors! Our hearts were beating fast and our minds running wild with imagination as we waited for the surprise to be disclosed.

Finally, the door was opened, and we were released. I led the pack as we ran in his direction, shouting, "Daddy!" He smiled from ear to ear as his three children ran toward him, calling his name. He pointed at our surprise. It was a wooden cart that he had attached to the back of his riding lawnmower. He had prepared a place for us to be with him! Full of excitement, we jumped in the wooden cart and readied ourselves for the expedition around our yard. Although we'd been in that same yard countless times before, never had it seemed that wonderful. Not once did any of us ask how long the ride would take, what direction we were going, or for the details of his intended path. We were content to simply be with him on a bumpy ride on that hot summer day. Relishing every moment, we were carefree, and we knew we were safe with our dad.

Although it was certainly a labor of his love, it also became a significant part of his weekend honey-do list! Our time in his lawn cart also gave my mom a few hours of much needed alone time, which, in hindsight, makes me wonder if she had been the mastermind of this endeavor after all!

Now that we are grown, we no longer run and jump into his lawn cart, but we do jump into his truck for what he has coined, "Windshield time." Windshield time means riding down the road, enjoying each other's company while looking ahead at nothing in particular. Sometimes, we discuss life's issues, and other times we laugh as he rehearses a new joke, or retells the same jokes that he's been telling us for forty years or so. Windshield time has, without a doubt, created some of my favorite memories. Other times my dad connects on the phone. He calls me and says, "I don't want anything, just to hear my little girl's voice."

> **Knowing someone's heart releases you from worry and doubt, and you will find yourself jumping in without hesitation.**

When you grow within a healthy family unit, trust grows, and it isn't necessary to compile a laundry list of questions. Knowing someone's heart releases you from worry and doubt, and you will find yourself jumping in without hesitation. That's how I feel about my dad. He has earned unfailing trust from his children. From his lap to his cart, to his truck, to his phone calls, he has successfully created intimate, safe places where we can call on him for help, guidance, and direction. We love him, and we trust him.

ABBA, FATHER

Three times in the New Testament, the word *Abba* is used as an intimate way of saying Father or Daddy. Jesus and Paul use this word to express their deep trust and dependence on Father God. In Mark 14:36, Jesus says, "Abba, Father, all things are possible for You. Take this cup away from Me; nevertheless, not what I will, but what You will." Jesus shows us the magnitude of their relationship and how the trust would rise at the loneliest moments of His life. It's as if He says, "I know you can, Father, but I still trust you if you don't."

Twice Paul uses Abba to refer to our adoption as sons and daughters. Romans 8:15 says, "For you did not receive the spirit of bondage again to fear, but you received the Spirit of adoption by whom we cry out, 'Abba, Father.'" And Galatians 4:6 says, "And because you are sons, God has sent forth the Spirit of His Son into your hearts, crying out, 'Abba, Father!'" Understanding the gift of adoption He has given, and functioning as His offspring, opens our eyes to the Father's heart toward His own.

Children react in response to their need, not thinking beforehand, but simply crying out for help. They freely ask for assistance and guidance from those they love and whom they know loves them. As sons and daughters, fear of crying for our Daddy's help should never enter our thoughts; it should happen naturally, without thought or hesitation. As Jesus and Paul called to their Father in that childlike manner, His desire for us is to do so as well.

> **"** *Allowing Abba to adopt you and nestle you in His arms of love, brings unimaginable peace and safety.* **"**

There are many parallels between our earthly fathers and our heavenly Father, and we comparatively mirror them in our minds. How we view our earthly father often dictates how we view our heavenly Father. Matthew 7:11 compares the two, "If you then, being evil, know how to give good gifts to your children, how much more will your

Father who is in heaven give good things to those who ask Him!"

Maybe you never knew your father. Or maybe you can't describe your earthly father as loving and memorable. Maybe he was absent, aloof, or even abusive. If so, I'm sorry, and I pray that you can receive healing for any pain in your heart. But regardless of your past, it is beautiful to know that your heavenly Father is always present. Your heavenly Father is close by your side, and He longs for you to call on Him. Psalm 68:5 says He is the "[F]ather to the fatherless." Allowing Abba to adopt you and nestle you in His arms of love, brings unimaginable peace and safety. He fills voids that your heart has tried to forget. He loves you more than you can ever imagine.

The tender voice of the Father calls us to embrace the immense love He offers, and accepting His love will change every aspect of your life. That kind of love and absolute acceptance clings to the heart, creating a safe and trusting relationship. Abba longs for you to want Him, to be with Him, to need Him. Hearing your voice is His desire, and the knowledge that He is readily available fills any vacancy or void in your heart.

RISKY MOVES

Nothing makes the Father happier than hearing us call His name, and He is faithful to respond to our heartfelt cries for help. Psalm 50:15 says, "And call on me when you are in trouble; I will deliver you, and you will honor me" (CJB). We also see this kind of response at the name of His Son, Jesus:

> Then they came to Jericho. As Jesus and his disciples, together with a large crowd, were leaving the city, a blind man, Bartimaeus

(which means "son of Timaeus"), was sitting by the roadside begging. When he heard that it was Jesus of Nazareth, he began to shout, "Jesus, Son of David, have mercy on me!"

Many rebuked him and told him to be quiet, but he shouted all the more, "Son of David, have mercy on me!"

Jesus stopped and said, "Call him" (Mark 10:46-49 NIV).

Stepping out of the parameters of the status quo, Bartimaeus made a risky move and cried out the only name that could bring him help. Knowing that hearing His name would grab Jesus' attention, he shouted all the more. Jesus' name was called, and His glory was displayed. Bartimaeus received a supernatural touch, forever changing his circumstances. Every time Jesus is called, He is faithful; every time the Father is called, Abba responds. Our heavenly Father has unquestionably fostered dependence on Him, and we must trust that relationship enough to call on Him, even if it means taking a risk like Bartimaeus.

> *From our Father's vantage point, we are His little children reaching for help, reaching for comfort, reaching our arms to Him to pick us up and hold us tightly.*

From our Father's vantage point, we are His little children reaching for help, reaching for comfort, reaching our arms to Him to pick us up and hold us tightly. Age does not matter, and we never grow too old to need His warm embrace. Nothing can ever hold a candle to the love of our Father. Questioning if He will be disingenuous, untruthful, passive, belittling, or harsh with us is a product of an unfounded and senseless fear. These characteristics go against His nature and come from our enemy's endeavor to damage our trust with our Father. Our Abba has always been a trustworthy Father. Call to Him, reach for Him, and you will not be disappointed. His love will cover your deepest longing.

POWER IN THE NAME

People love to hear the sound of their name. During my teen years, Dad reinforced this truth and its importance. He studied Kevin Trudeau's *Mega Memory*, passing on his new techniques to the family. This was challenging for me because I seem to remember faces better than names. My husband often teaches the importance of name recognition also, suggesting that knowing someone's name gives them a sense of belonging.

Our oldest daughter nonchalantly began calling her grandfather by his first name instead of Grandpa. She had heard her grandmother calling him "Bob," so that's what she learned. We felt as if we needed to correct her, but her grandfather would not hear of it. With a knowing nod, he picked her up and said, "You can call me anything you want!" She set the standard, and "Bob" is what he is lovingly called by all our children. You see, he was delighted that she was calling for him and interacting with him. His first grandchild calling him by his name brought him such joy! She could ask him for anything, and he would respond affirmatively. Similarly, the Father speaks to David in Psalm 91:14-15 and says, "Because he holds fast to me in love, I will deliver him; I will protect him, because he knows my name. When he calls to me, I will answer him; I will be with him in trouble; I will rescue him and honor him" (ESV).

I have called on my Father's sweet name countless times and in countless situations, and, without exception, He has responded. There is one experience, however, that played out differently than I expected. While driving down the road late one night, my mind swirling with questions and sadness, intense fear overtook me. Utterly breathless, I was experiencing my first and only panic attack. I pray I never feel anything like that again! My mind and emotions were tossed around like a toy boat in the ocean, and every emotional wave made me feel helpless. For that moment, I did not know what to do, how to react, or where my Father was. Frozen in fear, I tried to say His name, but my tongue felt thick and useless. Knowing He would respond if only I could get the word out of my mouth, I continued fighting. I knew His name had the power to deliver, as Jeremiah 10:6 said, "No one is like you, Lord; you are great, and your name is mighty in power" (NIV).

> ❝ *I called His name, and He accomplished what I was incapable of doing on my own.* ❞

A few moments later, His sweet name finally passed my lips, and though I did not feel an immediate change in the atmosphere, I was on the correct path. The enemy, in full attack mode, was determined to thwart my efforts. As with Bartimaeus, it required perseverance, allowing nothing to hinder my cries; I pressed on. Gaining my boldness, I responded to Satan, "You can't seriously think I will stop!" Repeatedly calling the name of Jesus, the heaviness diminished, and glory replaced the darkness. I called His name, and He accomplished what I was incapable of doing on my own. In Romans 10:13, we read, "For 'everyone who calls on the name of the Lord will be saved'" (ESV). I was spent by the whole ordeal, but, in turn, amazed at His willingness to save His child when I cried out to Him.

UNBELIEVABLE INHERITANCE

Because we are His children, He has given us all authority, rights, and ownership, through His name. John 1:12 explains our inheritance, "But to all who did receive him, who believed in his name, he gave the right to become children of God" (ESV). What belongs to the Father belongs to His offspring. This reminds me of my dad's view on his children's shared ownership with him and how adamantly he feels about the subject.

Shortly after I began driving, my parents purchased a gray Mitsubishi truck for me to use until I could buy my own vehicle. One day I asked them, "Can I tell people the truck belongs to me?" My mom felt that it would be dishonest, but Dad had a different way of looking at the situation. "If she can say this is her house, then she can say it's her car. If my name is on the deed, then it belongs to her," he said.

What belongs to your Father belongs to you as well. Allow that truth to jolt your thinking. Like a lightbulb turning on in your mind, let it illuminate the reality of sonship and transform how you view yourself. You are His child, and He is your Father, and no father can compare. In Isaiah 43:1, He declares, "Fear not, for I have redeemed you; I have called you by your name; you are mine" (ESV). What belongs to the Father belongs to His children!

" *What belongs to the Father belongs to His children!* "

Paul describes beautifully in Romans 8:15-17, the Father's heart for His children, and the unbelievable inheritance He will provide for His family.

> This resurrection life you received from God is not a timid, grave-tending life. It's adventurously expectant, greeting God with a childlike "What's next, Papa?" God's Spirit touches our spirits and confirms who we really are. We know who he is, and we know who we are: Father and children. And we know we are going to get what's coming to us—an unbelievable inheritance! We go through exactly what Christ goes through. If we go through the hard times with him, then we're certainly going to go through the good times with him! (MSG).

AN IDENTITY THAT STICKS

Recognizing the importance of names, my parents thought long and hard about what to name their children. Decisions were made, and our forever identities were claimed. Along with our names, Dad gave a blessing to each of us, a personal gift from our earthly father. For myself, he said, "You will always be adored, and not just by me." For Farah, "You will be happy and prosperous, and your children will rise and call you blessed." Lastly, for Aaron, "God is your portion." Throughout our lives, we have seen the evidence and confirmation of these blessings on countless occasions. For instance, some of the first words my husband said to my dad while shaking his hand were, "Your daughter is adorable." Dad immediately went home and informed my mom, "Well, Vickie, I just met our son-in-law." Just a simple phrase, yet it was powerful in thwarting fear and giving my parents perfect peace when we decided to marry.

Not only did my dad give us names and blessings, he also enjoys giving a new nickname to people he meets. It may be from his first impression or a story that is told, but he will customize a new identity for that person. I could ramble on forever with all the names he has coined through the years. If he likes you, you will inevitably receive a name from Dad. Well, you will more than likely get one if he doesn't like you as well, but we won't go there. But if he gives you a name, it will latch on and forever be a connector between you and him.

> **He has always had a forever name for you, an identity that sticks regardless of circumstances or your mistakes.**

When you call on the name of your heavenly Father, He also gives you a name, different from what the world calls you, and the opposite of what the enemy has tried to make you accept. Isaiah 49:1b says, "The LORD called me from the womb, from the body of my mother he named my name" (ESV). He has always had a forever name for you, an identity that sticks regardless of circumstances or your mistakes. Isaiah 62:2b-4 gives us insight into the feelings Abba has for His children:

You will be called by a brand-new name, given to you from the mouth of Yahweh himself. You will be a beautiful crown held high in the hand of Yahweh, a royal crown of splendor held in the open palm of your God! You will never again be called the Abandoned One, nor will your land be called Deserted. But you will be called My Delight Is in You (TPT).

Don't allow yourself to be misidentified. Who you were and what you were tethered to in the past, simply stated, vaporizes as a puff of smoke. He created for you a brand new identity when you became His child. Your name is given to you by your Father. You are who He says you are.

TRUST ABBA

Without reservation, Abba leads our lives into a culmination of compliance and unity with Him. Our Father is unwavering and loyal to the bone. Why? Because we are His, and He is faithful. John 10:14 assures us of the Father's feelings toward us, "I am the good shepherd. I know my own and my own know me" (ESV).

Amid turmoil, we can thrive and believe, because we know He responds when we call on His name. Unfazed at the fiery darts thrown our way, we push forward with faith and determination. Satan may continue his tirade of accusations and fear; still, we trust. We see through his tactics and temptations. The enemy may give the appearance of isolation, but we are never alone in this fight. Our Father is waiting to engage as soon as we call out, "Abba!"

With bumps along the journey, let's call on His name and go for a ride! No need for questioning—How long will this take? What direction are we going? or What is your plan? We trust and enjoy the ride, in perfect peace, knowing our Father is in control. No, we didn't start with this confidence. We developed it after He proved Himself trust-worthy many times over. With this confidence, we do not need instruments of carnal warfare, but as Psalm 20:7 says, "We trust in the name of the LORD our God" (ESV).

3
Trust When Tempted

*You are tempted in the same way that everyone
else is tempted. But God can be trusted not to let you be
tempted too much, and he will show you how to escape
from your temptations*
(1 Corinthians 10:13 CEV).

If I wasn't with my dad on Saturdays growing up, I was with my best friend, Jennifer. We lived beside each other for almost all my childhood and teen years. We were adventurous little girls and always wanted to be outside playing until the sun set. The outdoors offered us a myriad of possibilities, and rainy days put a damper on all our plans. One dreary Saturday, full of disappointment, we opted to play in the garage that her parents had recently renovated. On the corner table sat a barrel cactus that had caught my eye. We had been cautioned that the spines could hurt and told it was strictly off-limits. However, my thoughts were swimming with questions, "How would I ever know if I didn't try? Why did she not want us to touch it? Surely, this small plant could not be that dangerous."

I imagine these were some of the same thought processes that Eve talked herself through, before caving to temptation. And just as with Eve, all the whys and why nots got the best of me. I had to touch the cactus! I knew the risks, but I was overcome by the urge to touch the forbidden plant, and I gave in to the pressure. And of course, the rest of the afternoon was spent with Jennifer's mother and a pair of tweezers, instead of a day full of play and excitement. What a nuisance and irritation I must have been! Curiosity always got the best of me. Even when responding to the Lord, I was no different. Why not, Lord? Why here, Lord? Why me, Lord? Why not me, Lord?

 Jesus gives us the blueprints to follow when battling the enemy's temptations.

The consequences of the cactus were painful. I was embarrassed, ashamed, and I just felt stupid. The purpose of the *no* was cautionary and protective. Jennifer's mother was attempting to keep pain and heartache far from our lives. But it was almost as if I had cataracts clouding my vision so that I couldn't see the purpose and importance of the *no*.

SAME OLD TACTICS

The enemy works in constant rotation—scheming and plotting against the children of God with the same temptation cycle. Opening our spiritual eyes, we can see his masquerade of pretenses. Once we recognize the cycle, we see the glaring repetition every time. Same old stuff, different day. Jesus gives us the blueprints to follow when battling Satan's temptations.

Matthew 4:1-11 says:

Then Jesus was led by the Spirit into the wilderness to be tempted by the devil. After fasting forty days and forty nights, he was hungry. The tempter came to him and said, "If you are the Son of God, tell these stones to become bread." Jesus answered, "It is written: 'Man shall not live on bread alone, but on every word that comes from the mouth of God.'" Then the devil took him to the holy city and had him stand on the highest point of the temple. "If you are the Son of God," he said, "throw yourself down. For it is written:

"'He will command his angels concerning you,
and they will lift you up in their hands,
so that you will not strike your foot against a stone.'"

Jesus answered him, "It is also written: 'Do not put the Lord your God to the test.'"
Again, the devil took him to a very high mountain and showed him all the kingdoms of the world and their splendor. "All this I will give you," he said, "if you will bow down and worship me."

Jesus said to him, "Away from me, Satan! For it is written: 'Worship the Lord your God, and serve him only.'"

Then the devil left him, and angels came and attended him (NIV).

Our opinionated enemy loves the sound of his voice. He poses as a powerful tyrant, working with our insecurities to sway our beliefs and detour us from the Word of God. His main objective is to sidetrack our spiritual disciplines, which leaves us in a weak and anemic state. We find ourselves in a place we never thought we would be—a place where our Father is no longer the priority. This lack of spiritual nutrition makes us vulnerable to Satan's attacks. In this position, we will succumb to the same three temptations he threw at Jesus, because we no longer are equipped with the Word to defy him.

These three temptations are often characterized as the lust of the eyes, the lust of the flesh, and the pride of life. They are explained by John this way in 1 John 2:15-17:

> Don't love the world's ways. Don't love the world's goods. Love of the world squeezes out love for the Father. Practically everything that goes on in the world—wanting your own way, wanting everything for yourself, wanting to appear important—has nothing to do with the Father. It just isolates you from him. The world and all its wanting, wanting, wanting is on the way out—but whoever does what God wants is set for eternity (MSG).

THE SPIRIT'S NUDGE

My great-great-grandfather, Cowan Russell, had built a small tin building on the property behind his home. He was a farmer and entrepreneur by trade, but he had a heart for the Lord and prayer. The building, approximately 24 x 40 feet in size, had a maximum capacity of only 40-50 people. Though it was small, he had a vision for what God could accomplish within its walls. It served as a gathering place for Bible studies, prayer meetings, and church services.

In the early '70s, a female Pentecostal evangelist began holding a revival in the small, tin building. She was a fiery preacher, and God was moving nightly in healings and powerful demonstrations of His Spirit. The meetings continued for several months, affecting the community and bringing upheaval to the enemy's plans. The preacher lived with her husband, son, and daughter in an RV camper, which they pulled behind their pickup truck. A power cord that ran from the tin building provided their electricity. It was not an elaborate way of living, but the Father had been faithful to provide for this little family.

My parents had been married for only a short time, and Mom regularly attended the revival services in that makeshift church house; however, Dad's work schedule made it difficult for him to be as involved. He pulled the noon to midnight shift as a truck dispatcher and a dock foreman at Associated Transport in Knoxville, Tennessee. Around 11 o'clock one morning on his way to work, he passed the evangelist's RV and felt he needed to give them $20. That being his gas and expense money for the week, he questioned his feeling and decided to wait.

> **"** *I wonder how many times we have talked ourselves out of obedience, out of God's will, and out of seeing the miraculous.* **"**

As the day went on, the Spirit continued to nudge him, and this family weighed heavily on his heart and mind. By the time he left work, it was 1:30 in the morning, and he had thought about that family all day. He knew what he needed to do, but he still hesitated, reasoning with God and debating with his inner man. He questioned the Father: "What if it's just my imagination and not You? What if I'm rejected? What will they think of me? What if I'm off base on this one?" We have all been guilty of allowing these questions to bombard our thoughts when we are asked to do uncomfortable things for the Lord. I wonder how many times we have talked ourselves out of obedience, out of God's will, and out of seeing the miraculous. We rationalize our way right out of victory. What have we missed out on because of our lack of trust in His voice?

It was now 2:30 in the morning, and Dad was on his way home from a long workday and still could not shake the feeling. He began to pray and ask God for a sign, "Okay, Lord, if this is what you want me to do, then when I drive by their camper, let an interior light be on. Then I will stop. If not, I will know it's just me and my imagination, and not You." His plan was in place, and it allowed his daunting feelings an escape route.

AN UNWANTED CHARACTER

As he drove on, he passed a large rock quarry with a gravel entranceway, and there stood a woman waving both arms wildly as if to flag him down. Slowing long enough to notice she was beautiful, wearing tight-fitting clothes, and smiling, he knew something was terribly wrong. There were no cars around, and he had a creepy feeling that she was up to no good. He passed her by but immediately decided not to leave her stranded. He hit his brakes and looked in the rearview mirror, but she was nowhere to be found. He looked around the entire area, but, to his surprise, there was no one. It was as if she had vanished. Thankfully, he sped up and continued with what God had put on his heart. Undoubtedly, the enemy was making every attempt he could to detour the assignment. He attacked his confidence; he worked feverishly against his thoughts; he even endeavored to use a seductive spirit to derail the plan God had set into motion.

The more I thought about this story, the more questions I had for the Lord. The woman seemed an unlikely, unannounced, and unwanted character. Why was she there? I thought long and hard about leaving her out of the narrative, but the Lord would not let me. I needed understanding, and He revealed to me the cycle of temptation. It is the same pattern Satan continues to use against God's people, and the same pattern he used against God's Son in Matthew 4: Lust of the flesh, the lust of the eyes, and pride of life. When we can recognize his manipulative nature and have spiritual eyes to see his schemes, we will be victorious.

Again, the key to victory over the enemy is the Word; and as Jesus said, "It is written," so should we. King David understood the power over temptation is the Word of God when he wrote Psalm 119:11, "I have hidden your word in my heart that I might not sin against you" (NIV).

Now I could see the pattern. The enemy was rearing his ugly head, spewing venomous lies, in a last-ditch effort to persuade my dad off course. Vexing him with tempting thoughts like, "You and your new wife need that money more than they do."—Lust of the eyes. "How do you know that was God, and not you?"—Pride of life. When his mind is too sharp for the venom, he came after his heart with a seductive spirit.—Lust of the flesh.

We often find ourselves in similar circumstances, because the enemy regurgitates the same old tactics over and over. Luke 4:13 warns, "When the devil had finished all this tempting, he left him *until* an opportune time" (NIV, emphasis added). He has every intention of coming back and trying again. He is a persistent foe. He waits, like a lion ready to pounce on his prey, until the most opportune time. Listen to Peter's caution to God's children in 1 Peter 5:8: "Be on your guard and stay awake. Your enemy, the devil, is like a roaring lion, sneaking around to find someone to attack" (CEV).

Enemies inevitably pursue. That should be no surprise. How we handle the attack determines the outcome. Our Father has given us an exit strategy and has put the weapons we need to win in our arsenal. Psalm 60:12 empowers us: "With God's help we will fight like heroes and he will trample down our every foe!" (TPT).

> " *Enemies inevitably pursue. That should be no surprise. How we handle the attack determines the outcome.* "

When tempted, we will press on with the Word, saying as Jesus did, "It is written." We will press on with prayer, as Jesus taught His disciples in Luke 22:40b, "Pray that you will not fall into temptation" (NIV). And we will vehemently stay alert to the enemy's conniving ways, and our Father will fight for us! Paul tells us in Romans 16:20, "And the God of peace will swiftly pound Satan to a pulp under your feet! And the wonderful favor of our Lord Jesus will surround you" (TPT). What a promise from the Father! When we focus on Him, He easily fights our battles.

THE HOLY SPIRIT'S DECISIVE VICTORY

In those moments of questioning, the Holy Spirit faithfully brings beautiful comfort and reassurance, as if to say, "I heard your prayer and will answer." As Dad drove by the camper, not only was one light on but every light, inside and outside of the home was turned on—every light. There was no doubt God was in this, but still stalling, he drove home and started getting ready for bed. As he turned the covers down, he remembers saying to himself, "I can't be-lieve this." He filled mom in on the details and said, "Vick-ie, do you want to go?" With an expectation to see what God was up to, she threw on her housecoat, house shoes, and got in the car.

As they approached the lit-up camper, they could hear praying and crying out to God from inside. Red-faced from tears, the preacher opened the door. Dad began shar-ing with them what God had put on his heart and what he had prayed. The couple had desperately been believing God for a miracle of financial provision. Seventeen dollars and some change were due the next morning, and they had no way of paying off the debt. Dad's twenty dollar expense money would cover the need and leave them some extra. He was seeing his Father's faithfulness, but He had more up His sleeve. This was only the beginning.

As the couples rejoiced, my parents could hear the cries of a child in the back room. They explained that their son, approximately eleven years old, had been helping load a hay wagon earlier in the day. He tried catching a bale of hay to prevent it from falling off the wagon, and, in the process, he broke his wrist. The little guy had been crying in pain for several hours. His wrist was twisted, swollen to larger than the width of his hand, and there was an appar-ent dip in the bone. My dad said, "I am taking him to the hospital now!" With unwavering faith, the preacher boldly declared, "If God can provide the financial need, then He can easily heal my boy." The atmosphere was charged as the four adults circled the young boy and began praying. Dad describes what he saw next as, "a horror story in reverse." He watched as the boy's wrist shrank, and the bone went perfectly into position. Instantly, the boy began laughing. He ran back to his younger sister and said, "It doesn't hurt anymore!" The preacher then put on her robe and house shoes, to match my mom, and said, "We are going to celebrate! Let's go to Waffle House with the extra two dollars."

OBEDIENCE TRUMPS TEMPTATION

Has going about your business and not listening to the Father's guidance become your norm? Is it His, yours, or the enemy's voice you are listening to? Your foe tries to suffocate you with temptation on your way to victory. He shouts doubt, fear, and contradictions to God's Word. On the contrary, your Father is sturdily standing beside you, whispering His loving instructions in your ear. It's your choice. Will you respond with obedience or take the devil's bait?

Regrettably, being tempted is a normal part of life in this world. Peter says in 1 Peter 4:12, "Dear friends, do not be surprised at the fiery ordeal that has come on you to test you, as though something strange were happening to you" (NIV). Testing times are common, and they are no stranger than waking, eating, or breathing.

Has going about your business and not listening to the Father's guidance become your norm?

At the earliest of ages, we are enticed to sin and disobey. When my youngest child, Tobie, was a preschooler, I worked diligently with him regarding "stranger danger." We role-played for weeks, practicing what he should do if someone he did not know approached him. We worked through every scenario I could conceive. With full assurance he was ready, I put together a plan with a friend of mine. It was test time.

At his older brother's football practice, while he was at the playground, she would offer Tobie candy and lure him into her van. I know this sounds crazy, but there was a lesson to be learned. I was convinced this would end with high fives and ice cream for his successful execution. However, I was shocked when he followed her without question into her van. I knew for sure he understood what to do, but, when tested, he failed. We had diligently rehearsed, but to my surprise, little Tobie took the bait. Sitting in the van and watching me walk toward him, he remembers thinking, "Oh no! I'm in trouble now!" I pretended to be unfazed and tried to make this a teachable moment. I officially introduced him to my cohort in crime and explained the magnitude of the situation.

If Tobie had heeded my warnings, we would have been sitting at a Baskin-Robbins, enjoying Rocky Road and Cake Batter ice cream, instead of sitting down to listen to a lecture. What exactly he was thinking, I'm not sure, but it appeared to me that we both went to bed quite discouraged that night. It was quite apparent that Tobie was not ready to conquer temptation. I could have second-guessed my efforts, but what-ifs are the worst: What if I had given Tobie more training? What if Eve had not listened to the serpent? What if I had trusted Jennifer's mom, and obeyed her instructions? What if Dad had not obeyed the voice of the Lord, and the little boy was not healed?

Because of the love of the Father, avoidance only works for a season, then we must deal with our mess. We are forced to open our eyes and see the truth. We must choose whom we will go to for help, support, and comfort. We must decide if we will move forward or digress. Obedience and trust are crucial to those decisions. Lurking pains and sins we thought were long since handled are lingering in the dark, ready to pounce at any time and bring torment.

These sins try to hold on and prolong their inevitable death, but they will die and bow to the Father, but only after you completely surrender.

It may seem like a tall order, but we must deal with our temptation and recognize the importance of obedience. In 1 Peter 2:8, Peter says of the untrusting, "They trip and fall because they refuse to obey, just as predicted" (MSG). A scot-free escape is not possible unless we are willing to obey the Father's instructions and let Him pound the enemy under our feet.

Lack of obedience is in direct correlation with a lack of trust.

Lack of obedience is in direct correlation with a lack of trust. You may ask, "Is my faith in His ability at maximum capacity?" A hard look at our actions will answer that question. I never realized I had a trust issue, but my actions begged to differ. If you asked me, I would say, "Yes, I trust Him! I have great faith!" I was trained well and knew the correct words to say, but when it came down to reality and true testing, I had to fight for my trust.

Training yourself to walk in obedience and to trust that your Father has your life in His beautiful hands, is when you soar with Him. You will live in His fullness and operate as one with your Father. Complete and total trust produces blessings. Sometimes it's a garden filled with fruit, a day filled with play, a plate filled with waffles, or a bowl filled with ice cream. It's our choice.

4
Trust During Training

*"Listen my friends, if we trust the LORD God and believe
what these prophets have told us,
the LORD will help us, and we will be successful"*
(2 Chronicles 20:20 CEV).

"Use good judgment and don't disappoint me," were
my dad's only two rules. I heard those words every time I made a decision, knowing full well
when I was making the wrong choice and disappointing
him. Shortly after getting my driver's license, I made one
of those wrong choices. It was a Sunday morning, and our
family was going berserk, running around, trying our best
to get out the door for church. I was agitated and annoyed
because I had been told I could not drive separately. Not
letting that stop me, I devised a plan.

As an Army veteran, being late was unacceptable for
my dad, of which I was very well aware. I knew that if I
took too long getting dressed, he would leave me behind.
There would be no other choice but for me to drive myself
to church. What could go wrong?

Not pleased or fooled by my plan, Dad left my room
with one stipulation, "Don't be late!" The only problem was
that now I had waited too long to get dressed and had no

idea how I could make it on time. After rushing through my final finishing touches, I ran and jumped into my truck and gunned it. My body jolted as I collided into Dad's truck that was parked behind mine, knocking it back six feet and rearranging the landscape timbers. Being late for church had just become the last thing on my mind!

With great trepidation, I drove to church. As I entered the foyer, I saw my sweet grandfather. I fell into his arms and dramatically explained the situation to my Papaw, ending with, "He's going to kill me!" Papaw escorted me gently back out to the parking lot to survey the damages. He softly smiled and said something I will never forget. He said, "Well, he's never killed you before, so I doubt he will today."

Hoping he forewarned my dad, I left the church the second the final prayer ended. I slowly drove back home and went to my bedroom. Dreading my punishment, I waited. I knew he was examining the damage and there was nothing I could do but take it like a champ. Calmly, he entered my room and said, "A new bumper, tailgate, and parts are not cheap, and you will pay every dime of damages." Trying my best to control my tears, I finally got out the words, "Yes, Sir." Not wanting me to be nervous about driving, he replied, "Don't ever drive in a hurry like that again. Dry your face and forget it." Then he added, "I will never admit how many times I've done worse."

My parents gave me a bill of two hundred dollars and allowed me to pay it back monthly. My job at the Christian bookstore at the local mall helped me pay off my debt. It pained me each time I handed over the payment; however, miraculously, I developed much better driving skills. Years later, my parents explained to me that the invoice I received was quite a bit different than the one *they* had received. Not only had they not charged me for labor, but dad had also instructed mom to put every penny I paid, slowly back into my account, making sure that I would not notice. It wasn't a matter of money; it was about learning. True, if they had said, "No big deal, we got this," I would have had the coolest parents on the planet. My driving skills, however, would not have improved, nor would I have expanded my knowledge of managing budgets. Experience is often the most effective teacher. You can hear something over and over, but until you experience it, you never master that skill.

SUPERSIZE ME

God provides training grounds that stretch us and prepare us for life and our calling. He orchestrates and aligns these times of training, to catapult us into Holy Spirit-given assignments. Once He has set the stage, He must prepare us.

> *God provides training grounds that stretch us and prepare us for life and our calling.*

In April 1992, McDonald's fast food started the supersize option for fries and drinks. Customers' large drinks could be increased by 10 ounces, and their fries by 1 ounce. The success, however, took a turn in 2004, when movie director Morgan Spurlock did an experiment where he ate nothing but McDonald's food for an entire month. If an employee asked if he wanted to supersize his meal, he had to say yes. The idea was to see how it would affect his body and to compare medical results from before and after the experiment. The drastic differences in his body and how he felt were staggering at the end of the month. As a result of the documentary, people became increasingly aware of their health, and McDonald's responded by making changes to the menu.

Watching Spurlock's journey made me think about the dedication and diligence this required of him. His willingness to sacrifice his desires and comforts for the cause had made an impression. What if I applied that same thought process with my spiritual intake and saw how it affected my spiritual life at the end of a month? What could thirty days of sacrifice do for my spiritual wellbeing?

❝ *Training is of paramount importance in our lives, but there comes the point where we must be able to put into practice what we have learned and move into the destiny God has planned.* **❞**

Putting together a plan consisting of praying, fasting, reading the Word, and keeping the Lord at the forefront of my mind, I moved forward with expectation. I continually said, "Lord supersize Me," and I quoted Hebrews 11:6b, "He is a rewarder of those who diligently seek Him." That month He revealed His glory, proving He was worth every sacrifice. He met me and changed me. The before versus after outcome was remarkably noticeable, and I have never been the same since. I had spiritual disciplines in my life previously, but not to that extent, or with the same passion. It was without doubt, a God-called and ordained training to prepare me for His service.

Being raised in a pastor's home, my husband was accustomed to spiritual disciplines. He has endless stories of his dad praying and fasting, and of his mother sitting behind a piano, singing worship songs. It was a way of life for them, and it helped mold him into the man he is today. Training is of paramount importance in our lives, but there comes the point where we must be able to put into practice what we have learned and move into the destiny God has planned. Rob moved from observing spiritual disciplines to operating in them himself. He went from a season of training to authentic participation. We see this progress play out in the life of Joshua, as he advances from an assistant to the leader of more than two million people.

THE ARMORBEARER

Moses was a mighty leader. He persuasively led the children of Israel out of Egypt's grasp of bondage and slavery. God used him to part the Red Sea, feed His children, intercede for their lives, discipline their stubbornness, and hand-deliver His Law. With awe and enormous respect, we look at Moses as Israel's most famous deliverer. However, I find myself fascinated with his armorbearer. Joshua's story of servanthood and drive has always intrigued me.

Numbers 27:18-20 says,

> And the LORD said to Moses: "Take Joshua the son of Nun with you, a man in whom is the Spirit, and lay your hand on him; set him before Eleazar the priest and before all the congregation, and inaugurate him in their sight. And you shall give some of your authority to him, that all the congregation of the children of Israel may be obedient."

God gave leadership and authority to Joshua, but not before he had proven his trust, loyalty, determination, and diligence.

WHAT SET HIM APART?

I am convinced that one of God's greatest pleasures comes from men and women who purpose in their hearts to experience Him in a real and passionate way. No matter what it takes, they pursue Him. Joshua trusted the Lord and set His mind like flint on the pursuit of knowing Him. He purposed in his heart to not look back until he knew God personally. The first time we see Joshua in Scripture is in Exodus 17:9. By this point, he had already won the confidence of Moses. Moses had chosen Joshua to lead a volunteer army against the Amalekites. His first time on the scene, he is recognized as a trustworthy and influential leader. And yet he was a man under authority. Allowing yourself to come under submission to those the Lord has put over you, and trust they have the best intentions for your life, is the best training ground for successful leadership.

When I think of Joshua, I instantly think of Steven, a fourteen-year-old young man who gave his heart to the Lord under our ministry. He was zealous to serve the Lord and my husband, immediately endearing himself to us. He was always available and ready to serve in any way he could. Several years later, he was hired as Rob's assistant and served in that role faithfully. The Holy Spirit sends people like Joshua and Steven to help and assist leaders, but their time of service also provides invaluable training ground for them as well. When you trust your leader and say "Here's what I have to offer, use me, train me, stretch me," you grab the heart of God.

Moses was inundated with continuous complaints, qualms, and suspicions from his people. Joshua must have been a refreshing presence in his life! Although we do not have the back story of how their friendship developed, we see their relationship worked. It may be that Moses knew him and his character firsthand, or perhaps someone had told him Joshua was an up-and-comer. The Lord, however, did make it clear to Moses when He directly spoke to him about Joshua. Their relationship took off and Joshua was not only trusted as the leader of his army but also a confidant for Moses. Exodus 17:9-10 says, "Moses said to Joshua, 'Choose us some men and go out, fight with Amalek. Tomorrow I will stand on the top of the hill with the rod of God in my hand.' So Joshua did as Moses said to him, and fought with Amalek. And Moses, Aaron, and Hur went up to the top of the hill." So, Joshua defeated Amalek and his people with the edge of the sword. With deep appreciation for one another, the two beautifully worked in tandem, accomplishing the plans of the Father for His people. What a correlation: Moses, interceding as he lifts the banner to encourage Israel's warriors, and Joshua, defeating their enemy with the sword.

God was making an indelible mark on the people's minds as He set up His next leadership. Moses saw Joshua as a leader, but the people needed to see him in that role also. He had to wait, learn, and gain respect before branching out as their leader. God in His infinite wisdom knows exactly which season we are about to enter. Because He knew the people of Israel were about to enter into a season of war, He elected the new leader, Joshua, a military commander, to lead His people. Don't question the season you are currently in. God has not abandoned you. Maybe He has you in a training ground, equipping you for your next season and readying you for His glory.

David had to go through the same training process, waiting while his favor grew in the eyes of man. After being anointed as king, he ran in circles for years before receiving the crown and walking in kingly authority. Why wait? Why the process? Because the journey built patience, character, and trust with those who followed him. It's important to note, the time did not have to be perfect for him alone, but also for the people who followed him and would support him as king.

> **"*God has not abandoned you. Maybe He has you in a training ground, equipping you for your next season and readying you for His glory.*"**

Trust while learning is difficult, but the Father gives you the strength you need to fulfill your training and graduate to the next level. Time in His presence is key to advancement in the Kingdom. Having a developed, stable, and secure relationship with the Father is a must for acceleration. Joshua gives us a perfect example to follow in Exodus 33:11: "So the LORD spoke to Moses face to face, as a man speaks to his friend. And he would return to the camp, but his servant Joshua the son of Nun, a young man, did not depart from the tabernacle." Though his position would require him to follow Moses back to camp, Joshua lingered at the Tabernacle.

URGENT PERSISTENCE

The Tabernacle represented the presence of God, the designated location to encounter glory. Although Joshua did not see God face-to-face as Moses had, he was closer than anyone else. Can you imagine being in his shoes? I doubt you would want to leave that environment either. I visualize Joshua stalling, waiting for Moses to permit him to linger. Maybe Moses saw his urgency. Perhaps they made eye contact, and Moses understood as he remembered the time he was in the holy place where he took off his shoes, and was awestruck by God's glory. He gave a look that said, "Take all the time you need. You need Him more than I need you right now." Knowing this moment could bring real, life-altering change, Moses saw this time with the Lord would train, teach, and equip Joshua more than he ever could.

You see, this was not the first time Joshua experienced this awe-inspiring power and presence of God. Exodus 24:13-14 explains how together he and Moses ascended the mountain of God. "So Moses arose with his assistant Joshua, and Moses went up to the mountain of God. And he said to the elders, 'Wait here for us until we come back to you.'" Joshua went farther up that mountain than any other man besides Moses. For six days, a cloud covered the mountain. On the seventh day, God called Moses out of the cloud, and Joshua waited for forty days. We see the two of them descend the mountain together in Exodus 32:17.

Joshua found himself a suitable spot to make camp, settled in, and waited on his leader. What a view he must have had. I often wonder what he saw, heard, and felt during that time. You have to know it was amazing. Exodus 19:18 tells us, "Mount Sinai was completely in smoke, because the Lord descended upon it in fire. Its smoke ascended like the smoke of a furnace, and the whole mountain quaked greatly." The earth shook when God stepped on the scene. Psalm 68:8 confirms, "The earth shook; The heavens also dropped rain at the presence of God; Sinai itself was moved at the presence of God, the God of Israel." The mountain moved in worship to the Most High God, and Joshua felt it tremble!

The earth responds to the glory of God. The Creator, whose feet daily touched its soil in Eden, was forced to suffer His absence as a consequence of sin. *The Passion* version beautifully paraphrases Romans 8:20-22:

For against its will the universe itself has had to endure the empty futility resulting from the consequences of human sin. But now, with eager expectation, all creation longs for freedom from its slavery to decay and to experience with us the wonderful freedom coming to God's children. To this day we are aware of the universal agony and groaning of creation, as if it were in the contractions of labor for childbirth.

The absence of His presence brings agony; and when that deficiency is filled, rejoicing flows, and in this case, the earth shook.

WALKING AWAY IS NOT AN OPTION

What an experience Joshua must have had! These occurrences can only satisfy temporarily, and then deep cries out to deep. Catching glimpses of glory but only being a spectator must have left him wanting. I thought for a moment about the longing for God that was building in Joshua, creating a desire that would not be satisfied with anything else in life. At times, I have watched God demonstrate His power through men and women, and longed for His presence to operate in my own life in that same manner. These moments thrust you into desperation, diligence, and determination to shift to a new level of intimacy with the Father.

I'm sure Joshua dreamed of his experience on the side of Mount Sinai often and had determined in his heart to never walk away from that presence again! That presence, I believe, is why Joshua would not leave the Tabernacle in Exodus 33:11. Walking away was not an option this time around. He knew the anointing made the difference in Moses' life, and he longed for that same anointing and power in his leadership. Joshua, the leader's assistant, would not depart from the Tabernacle—the presence of God. In verse 10 of chapter 33, we learn all the people could see from their tents, the pillar of cloud standing at the tent door of the Tabernacle, and they worshiped. They saw it; however, Joshua felt it. This time was different from all the other encounters, and he could not walk away. These are the moments that change us, train us, and transform us into the men and women God intends for us to be. These are the moments that forge an unbreakable bond that seals us with the Father. They don't just happen. We must go to the tabernacle. We must engage in His presence.

> ** " ** *Time spent with Him launches you into the places you cannot access on your own.* **"**

Time spent with Him launches you into the places you cannot access on your own. No one understood this better than King David. His success was a direct result of his trust and understanding of who was in charge, and who had the lead role. He had to trust God was going to fulfill His purpose, and willingly accept a subordinate role until his time was right. Tending sheep, being a delivery boy to his brothers, being a harpist for King Saul, and even running for his life, was his way of life for years after being anointed as king. David was willing to do the mundane, seemingly meaningless tasks, and serve faithfully while waiting to ascend to the throne. He could have easily gotten discouraged with this hodgepodge of tasks; however, each was part of his training to impart knowledge and to prepare him for his leadership.

Training grounds, persistence, and tabernacle experiences develop intimacy with the Father and make your heart ready for miracles, signs, and wonders. Both Joshua and David understood this. And though they may have questioned the seasons they found themselves in, they stayed the course, becoming major players in the story the Father was writing for His children.

> ❝ *Training grounds, persistence, and tabernacle experiences develop intimacy with the Father and make your heart ready for miracles, signs, and wonders.* ❞

I want to challenge you to read David's words in Psalm 63:1-8 as a prayer of intimacy, preparing your expectant heart for miracles and strengthening you with endurance if you find yourself currently in a training season:

> O God of my life, I'm lovesick for you in this weary wilderness. I thirst with the deepest longings to love you more, with cravings in my heart that can't be described. Such yearning grips my soul for you, my God! I'm energized every time I enter your heavenly sanctuary to seek more of your power and drink in more of your glory. For your tender mercies mean more to me than life itself. How I love and praise you, God! Daily I will worship you passionately and with all my heart. My arms will wave to you like banners of praise. I overflow with praise when I come before you, for the anointing of your presence satisfies me like nothing else. You are such a rich banquet of pleasure to my soul. I lie awake each

night thinking of you and reflecting on how you help me like a father. I sing through the night under your splendor-shadow, offering up to you my songs of delight and joy! With passion I pursue and cling to you. Because I feel your grip on my life, I keep my soul close to your heart (TPT).

5
Trust With Expectation

And those who know Your name will put their trust in You;
for You, Lord, have not forsaken those who seek You
(Psalm 9:10).

L ong before sunrise, my siblings and I, still yawning, crawled into the back of Dad's truck bed, where he had set a full-size mattress, blankets, pillows, books, and toys. He had created a welcoming environment that transformed our groggy beginnings. Finally, our Florida beach vacation was underway, and the three of us were brimming with excitement. The truck's topper shielded us from the wind and elements as we traveled down the interstate at 70 miles per hour. Several hours in, the excitement had died down somewhat, and we all fell sound asleep. I recall waking before my brother and sister, peering out the window of the topper, and hoping to catch a glimpse of the first palm tree. I knew when I saw one that our destination was close. Palm trees meant vacation and a week of family fun, so I loved them. While scanning the scenery for palms, I imagined my mom was riding in the front of the truck doing the same. Maybe she was just watching the panoramic landscape, but I knew she was thanking God for once again blessing our family with an opportunity to rest.

She had invested a great deal into this trip, and it was all she talked about for weeks. Hours of preparation for getaways are typical for most moms. Checklists a mile long to get a young family packed for an extended time are common. Her list, however, began differently than the norm. First and foremost on her list was prayer. She taught us to pray for everything imaginable, from the smallest of details to what most considered impossible. Vacations were no exception.

We had family friends who were in the market to sell their vacation timeshare, and, as Mom put it, "God gave it to us. He always makes a way." Now that we were owners, once a year we searched through the RCI book of destinations to pick our newest vacation spot. But of course, Mom said, "We have to pray and agree first that God will give us the perfect location for our family. We've worked hard and need a good vacation." Then she held that book and prayed for location, weather, travel conditions, any hindrances, and the supernatural ability to choose the perfect getaway. Mom, to this day, will tell you the only vacation we had that was not a success was the one she did not cover in prayer. For her, a family vacation was not merely fun, but it was also an answer to her prayers. That being said, I knew she was praising Him as we rode down I-75. Even if it was silent, she was praising.

Palm trees are still my favorite. They are reminders of the fun times in my life, and I believe they are one of God's favorites as well. Why else would He command the Tabernacle be decorated with them? We decorate our homes with our favorite items, so naturally, He must love palms as much or more than I do. Palm branches represent victory, joy, and freedom. His people waved them in the air shouting, "Hosanna!" as Jesus entered Jerusalem. Just as palm trees caused me to expect fun summer days, the palm branches were waved as they fully expected Him to deliver them from the Romans. Although He did not square off against their enemy as expected, He was good on His promise to deliver His people.

I believe He loves an expectant heart and finds joy when His children look for Him to do the miraculous. Andrew Murray, a South African pastor in the nineteenth century, said, "Faith expects from God what is beyond all expectation." Our analytical way of thinking can sometimes get in the way of the beautiful confidence He longs for us to have in Him. He has not and will not disappoint. Ephesians 3:20-21 speaks to this expectant view, "Now to him who is able to do immeasurably more than all we ask or imagine, according to his power that is at work in us, to him be glory in the church and in Christ Jesus throughout all generations, for ever and ever! Amen" (NIV).

> **Our analytical way of thinking can sometimes get in the way of the beautiful confidence He longs for us to have in Him.**

Ask anyone who has been associated with my mother, and they will agree that she demonstrates wild, outrageous faith and trust in her Father. She can be quite presumptuous, in an amazing way, that He will undoubtedly do what she requests. This attitude of, "He's got this, so sit back, relax, and watch what He will do," is intriguing to see play out. Her approach with Him has often reminded me of Mary, Jesus' mother, at the wedding in Cana of Galilee.

GLORY REVEALED

Mary demonstrated unflinching expectancy at this wedding when she looked at her Son and said, "They have no wine" (John 2:3). Did you notice she did not request anything? She just verbalized the problem and trusted Jesus to do the rest. This scripture makes me smile because I can visualize Mary as she shared this news with her Son. I know the look she gave Him because I have often given that same look to my boys. When I do, they know without a doubt that I am saying, "Fix this!" Jesus responded to His mother in verse 4, "Woman, what does your concern have to do with Me? My hour has not yet come." Again, I am amused with Mary as she seemed to ignore Jesus and began handing out instructions.

> His mother said to the servants, "Whatever He says to you, do it."
>
> Now there were set there six waterpots of stone, according to the manner of purification of the Jews, containing twenty or thirty gallons apiece. Jesus said to them, "Fill the waterpots with water." And they filled them up to the brim. And He said to them, "Draw some out now, and take *it* to the master of the feast." And they took it. When the master of the feast had tasted the water that was made wine, and did not know where it came from (but the servants who had drawn the water knew), the master of the feast called the bridegroom. And he said to him, "Every man at the beginning sets out the good wine, and when the guests have well drunk, then the inferior. You have kept the good wine until now!"
>
> This beginning of signs Jesus did in Cana of Galilee, and manifested His Glory, and His disciples believed in Him (John 2:5-11).

Learning to Trust the Father's Heart

Mary, unfazed by the situation, had absolute trust and faith in her Son, and she was not taking no for an answer. The way she carried herself, with such confidence and unwavering faith, is a beautiful example of the goal the Father has for us. She knew she could depend on her Son, and He would not let her down. I imagine Mary could not wipe the smile off her face as the wine was served. Her Son was responsible for saving the day, and she was in all likelihood ecstatic with His first public miracle.

On this wedding day, Mary was ready to show everyone what her Son was capable of doing. Doubt was not an option, for she had complete trust in His ability to fix the situation. She had no way of knowing the details of how He would accomplish this miracle, and yet her confidence in Him was evident. Her actions assure us that she never doubted or swayed in her belief in His capability. Mary demonstrated a trust that develops over time—the tested and proven experiential faith, where doubt is nowhere to be found.

" *Doubt was not an option, for she had complete trust in His ability to fix the situation.* **"**

With confidence, she said, "Whatever He says to you, do it." She did not say, "Not if it seems reasonable to you," or "If it makes sense in your mind," but she said, "Whatever He says, do it." She knew the result would be His manifested glory. We long for the supernatural and His glory in our lives; and Mary shows us the key to unlocking a relationship on that level. It takes complete trust. Whatever He says, do it!

Every time *glory* is revealed—every time. This first miracle developed faith and trust for the disciples. Little doubt remained after the wine, and this set them on a journey of belief. They would now live a life of expectancy.

THE ROCKING CHAIR

Just like Mary, my mom demonstrated the beauty of full expectation and belief in the Lord. This relationship was developed in her special place with the Father. She would spend hours praying in her rocking chair with her Bible; that rocking chair was her special place. I remember hearing her pray as I sat on the floor outside her bedroom, pressing my ear against the door, and trying to listen to their conversation. I wanted to hear her prayers because I knew they equaled power. She had taught me to have high expectations for what God would do through those prayers, and that miracles were always a possibility. She showed our family that raw dependence on the Father was the only option for a fulfilled life. I have often wondered what would have been if she had not spent that time in prayer for our family. I have many times said, "A rocking chair saved my life."

In every home we have ever lived in, I have followed her example and had a special place where I met with Him. It was our comfortable spot, where I could be genuine with my Father, and He would open up the heavens. I longed for this time, but, in the beginning, with small children, it was difficult to find.

I inquired of the Lord, asking how to fix the problem, and He answered, "You don't have to be alone to have your private time with Me." From then on, I approached my time with Him differently. It was okay if we were interrupted; my children were learning the importance of prayer, as I had learned from my mom. I prayed and worshiped, and they were right there with me, sometimes walking around me, or even over me, but they were learning spiritual disciplines. As they grew older, they viewed it as part of our daily routine. It became less difficult, and at times, they would join me in my worship.

> " *You don't have to be alone to have your private time with Me.* "

But one special day was different. As I prayed, I began hearing prayers being offered up that weren't mine, so I got up and started walking through the house. Robbie, our 14-year-old, was pacing the floor speaking in tongues. Eleven-year-old Lexi was anointing the rooms with oil, and nine-year-old Tobie was sitting on his bed writing a sermon under the anointing. It was an empowering sight. It gave me complete confidence that God was building faith in my children and that their expectancy would continue to flourish. He was hovering over their lives and birthing ministries and equipping my babies with authority! They were experiencing power in the secret place with their heavenly Father.

CHILDLIKE FAITH

My family's faith was not built only on Mom's prayers and Bible stories, but also on actual miracles that repeatedly took place in our lives. Both sets of my grandparents, my mom, and my dad have an endless supply of miraculous stories, and I knew them all very well. This included the healing of broken bones, skin cancers, tuberculosis, rheumatic fever, and pancreatitis. They also had stories of personal financial miracles and other ways that the Lord had supernaturally provided for them. For the adults in my life, absolutely nothing was beyond His ability, and I am forever grateful that none of them ever grew out of their "childlike faith."

I will always remember watching *The 700 Club* one day when I was in the fourth grade and had stayed home from school because of a stomach virus. At the end of each episode, the news anchors would pray, and words of knowledge would follow. Ben Kinchlow said, "A young girl is watching who stayed home from school today, God is healing your stomach." I knew it was me, and I jumped up and got ready for school. My mom simply smiled as I explained to the school secretaries that I was instantly healed. We got a few odd looks from them, but I did not care because I knew exactly what God had done for me.

We sincerely asked God before we tackled anything. When it was time to go shopping for new school clothes, we would sit in the parking lot of K-Mart and pray for good deals, guidance, and direction. All that was on my mind was how the people walking by must be thinking we were a bunch of weirdos. But, without fail, we left the store with Mom praising the Lord for His goodness to our family. Twice a year my mom, my younger sister, and I went to my Great Aunt Shirley's house for our hair permanents. She was a hairdresser and had her salon set up in the basement of her home. Of course, Mom prayed, "Lord we ask for no damage to our hair, we ask that the box we purchase is in good condition and nothing is missing, we ask that the curls turn out perfectly, and You would use Shirley during the process." She prayed for everything!

Mom had a God-given ability to create faith and expectation in her children. The thought that He would not do something never crossed our minds. Expectation, coupled with my wild imagination, was a recipe for endless hours of daydreaming. Boy, did I ever dream! I would dream about all He could do, when He would do it, and how He planned on using me to accomplish the miraculous. I never imagined an outcome other than victory.

SCANDALOUS RED SHOE

Mom's devotion and belief taught us to trust God when we prayed, and we would see miracles. One particular miracle was Mom's favorite to tell, and my favorite story to hear. It is extraordinarily special to her because it led to an intimate encounter with glory. It happened at a church in Maryville, Tennessee, when she was twelve years old. Her mother had insisted that she sit on the front row so that she could keep an eye on her. All Mom cared about was having an exit strategy for when she needed to go to the restroom because those night services could go on for hours. It did not bode well for her one night as she and her friend became trapped in that front row. They were wedged between the pew, her Aunt Audine's laid-out body, and at least five other Holy Spirit-filled women of God. Those girls were not going to move anytime soon.

Aunt Audine, who was then in her forties, had come to the altar to pray about pain in her back. This was undoubtedly not the first time she had petitioned God for this miracle. An understanding of her story, however, is significant in grasping the fullness of this account.

You see, my great aunt, Audine Russell Harmon, was one of eleven children. Before the government persuaded her father to cede their land to the National Park Service, they lived in Cades Cove, Tennessee. She was one-and-a-half years old when her siblings were jumping on their parent's antique poster bed, and she cried out to join in on the fun. The chain of events that followed had lasting consequences. Her little body was tossed around the bed like a rag doll. However, the children's joy quickly turned to fear when Audine hit one of the wooden posts as she soared through the air. Her screams made it well known that she was in the throes of agonizing pain. Her little cries and groans could be heard throughout the house for weeks. There were no doctors near where they lived in that remote area of the mountains, rendering her parents helpless.

As time passed, the Russells knew this would affect their little girl for life. The growth in her right leg and hip was stunted, and she had constant pain on that side of her body and in her back. The shoes she needed to correct the four-inch difference in her legs cost more than one hundred dollars. It might as well have cost a million dollars! There was no way the family could afford that, so she grew up limping around barefooted and walking on her tippy toes.

At twelve years old, she met a boy named Ed that her father had hired to help in the fields. They often sat on the front porch together talking, and a great friendship developed. Ed did not seem to mind her limp and promised to one day marry her and buy her first pair of shoes. Four years later, at sixteen, she stood barefoot at the altar. Ed got a job at ALCOA, Aluminum Company of America, and saved every extra penny he had until he could purchase her first pair of black, built-up shoes. These shoes lasted her more than 20 years. When it came time to replace them, Audine insisted on ordering a red pair. Red was scandalous in those days, and all her friends said that would be a foolish decision because they would not even match all her clothes. The wise thing to do was go with black again, but she loved color. She decided she did not care if she appeased her well-meaning friends or not. If that were the only pair she would have for years, they might as well be fabulous. My mom remembers being a young girl when Audine began wearing her new red shoes.

Now Mom found herself reluctantly sitting on the front pew of that church looking down on Audine, only inches away from those scandalous red shoes. For hours she lay there under the power of God, and prayers from those saints never ceased. As the women gathered to the right of Audine, Mom noticed her skirt moving, like a wind had caught hold of it, but there was no source from where the wind originated. No one was fanning. There was no air vent. No one was even touching her. Mom's annoyance about the restroom situation was the last thing on her mind. The wind of His glory was blowing, and people were taking notice.

Only inches from Mom, the red shoelace began blowing in that wind, and in a matter of seconds, everything would change. From Mom's bird's-eye view, she could see golf-ball sized knots slowly start at Audine's right hip, working down her leg to her foot, with a final push at her heel, as if God was stretching her. Each knot caused her leg to extend until her shoe popped right off. Mom began shouting, "Look, look! Oh, my God. Thank You, Jesus!" An eruption of praise broke out in that altar. Two women helped Audine sit up. When she realized what had happened, she jumped, danced, and rejoiced before the Lord, as the women around her replied with equal enthusiasm.

Healing in her back was what she had requested, but she received much, much more. As Paul tells us in Ephesians 3:20, God is able to exceed our greatest expectations. He was faithful and did exceedingly and abundantly above all she could ever think or imagine. Audine, Mom, and the people present would never forget that night. Her story has been passed down from my mom to her children, and, for that matter, to anyone Mom thought could benefit. Interestingly, after the healing, the Lord allowed the smallest of limps to remain, and Ed questioned, "Why would God do that much and not the rest?" Someone said it was for her testimony, and for the rest of her life, she testified!

As they prepared to leave the church, Ed asked if she wanted to put the shoes back on, and she said, "Are you kidding me, I will never wear those things again." He held her shoes, as she walked barefoot out of the church just as she had on her wedding day. Having only owned two pairs of shoes for forty plus years of her life, and having a love for fashion, she had a closet to fill! When she passed away, she owned over 200 pairs of shoes, every color, shade, and style.

It is worth noting that she kept one shoe in storage, and my mom asked her for that red shoe as a sign of the supernatural. From time to time, I will pull out that scandalous red shoe and thank the Father for supernatural interruptions in our lives. I have determined in my heart to not squander this gift of expectation that has been handed down to me and commit to continue to share His glory. What a family heirloom to pass to your children—the miraculous. Telling these precious stories allows God to build my children's young faith and trust in their heavenly Father.

OUR SONG

As a little girl, the palm trees caused expectancy to rise in my heart, as a sign of what was to come. When Mary saw a need for wine, expectancy rose in her heart, and she witnessed a miracle. When Audine longed for the miraculous, her expectation was taken to new levels, and wild faith rose in a young girl's heart. Expectancy is not difficult to build when trust is at work in our lives. We know our Father will show up and showcase His glory on our behalf because He

Learning to Trust the Father's Heart

has shown us with His actions. Interestingly, when it comes to the conversation of expectancy and trust, the Lord again calls my attention to a special memory I have with my dad.

As I rested my elbows on the cool windowsill, cupping my chin in my little hands, I waited for his car to enter our neighborhood. "He's home! He's home!" I squealed as I ran toward the front door. Standing on the third step in our split-level home, making me somewhat closer to his face when the door opened, I jumped up and down with expectancy. *What will he bring me today?* I wondered. Then the moment I had waited for all day finally was here, Daddy was home. Both of us blissfully smiled from ear to ear as he asked, "Do you have a song for me today?" I belted out the simple song he had written and I had sung to him daily for as long as I could remember.

> When my daddy gets home, I check his pockets,
> When my daddy gets home, I check his pockets,
> I'm going to check them just to see if there's anything for me
> When my daddy gets home, I check his pockets.

Then the game began. "Well which pocket is your surprise in today, I wonder?" he would tease while I scrambled to find my surprise. Daily he brought some special trinket: a stick of gum, candy, pen or pencil, a poem or song he had written. It was nothing significant as far as price was concerned, but it was huge in my heart. Moments like this with my father hardwired me with a natural slant toward trust. His actions proved his faithfulness.

 Expectancy is not difficult to build when trust is at work in our lives.

Expectancy does not equal understanding! On the contrary, it is surrender and total reliance on the Father when you face desperate situations. Changing your perspective, amid pain and uncertainty, allows you to see the situation as a miracle in the making, a sign of what is coming. This is trust and faith in action, not seeing and still believing.

6
Trust When You're Afraid

When I am afraid, I put my trust in you
(Psalm 56:3 NIV).

If asked what memory stands out most to me from my younger years, I would answer without a doubt, my first trip to Disney World. At only nine years old, I felt that I had awaited this trip for a lifetime. Our family, along with some of our dearest friends, had planned for months to ensure that everything went off without a hitch. The sweltering Florida heat did not hinder our enthusiasm to conquer every game, show, and ride. By the end of the day, one ride remained. At the sight of it, I was transformed from my previously brave self into a skittish coward. Hiding behind my mom, I was suddenly prepared to call it a night. I stood at the base of that Ferris wheel, my neck hurting as I strained to see the top, thinking, *I can't, and I won't do this.*

Pushing past my nerves, I climbed into the cart with our friends on this risky venture. My heart was pumping out of my chest. The higher we climbed the more jittery I became. Then, to my dismay, our cart stopped at the very top. Sitting there high above the park, my dad's friend menacingly began shaking the cart, and sheer panic set in. While the other two children howled with laughter, my little sister and I were beside ourselves with fear. With a distressed look on my face and tears streaming down hers, we made our feelings well-known. Fear had sunk its claws in deep. We couldn't get off that Ferris wheel quickly enough. To this day, my sister and I struggle with the fear of heights.

On my daughter Lexi's 16th birthday, she and her friends pushed me to overcome that fear! The Island, in Pigeon Forge, Tennessee, has a 200-foot-tall Ferris wheel, that I reluctantly agreed to ride with the girls. Although I would much rather have been firmly planted on the ground, I took a leap of faith. I kept my eyes closed through the entire ride, held my daughter's hand, and listened to worship music. I endured the experience but what a sad spectacle I must have been. I hated every second of it and will never do it again. Feeling suspended in mid-air brings me no joy, but that wasn't the point. Pushing through my fear, regardless of how I was feeling and demonstrating boldness to my daughter carried more weight than my apprehensions.

Fear has had more of a place in my life than I am happy to admit. Sadly, many times I listened to the enemy more than my loving Father, making my ministry ineffectual. Night terrors and tormenting dreams meant to stop my calling were commonplace. Satan's attempts to bind fear around my throat, with full intent, not only to take my voice but also to take my calling, seemed inescapable. Nevertheless, in the back of my mind, the startling idea of my enemy using my fear to defeat my calling sickened me. I earnestly sought my Father to help me regain my brave disposition and confidence and to help me fight against crippling fear. Let Proverbs 29:25 soak into your spirit: "Fear and intimidation is a trap that holds you back. But when you place your confidence in the Lord, you will be seated in the high place" (TPT).

MUMMY GAME

Toilet paper, believe it or not, is a necessary tool for youth pastors. I would argue that more games are played in youth facilities with toilet paper than with any other item. Put a roll in the hands of creative youth pastors, and the possibilities are endless. You can see their minds reeling with ridiculous notions, as smiles instantly appear on their faces. My husband was the king of fun-time games as a youth pastor. He loved coming up with new contests, races, and ways to loosen up the crowd. One game in his rotation was the mummy game. He split the students into groups. He picked one to be the mummy, while several others gathered around. All were armed with rolls of toilet paper and were chomping at the bits to "mummify" their friend before the other teams. The mummy stood still while teammates wrapped him up in toilet paper, and the crowd cheered them on.

" *If given permission, the enemy will thoroughly wrap us up in every kind of fear imaginable, until we become virtually indistinguishable from a mummified corpse.* "

The mummy game, used for fun, creates a vivid picture of the constraint fear can eerily wrap us in. If given permission, the enemy will thoroughly wrap us up in every kind of fear imaginable, until we become virtually indistinguishable from a mummified corpse. Fear opens a door labeled *security*. Convincing us that playing it safe is the way to go, we cautiously walk through the door only to find ourselves wrapped up like the mummy. Being wrapped in debilitating fear hinders our movement, speech, and hearing. Rather than moving forward, we stay stuck in one position. Because the layers of fear are pressed tightly against our ears, we are motionless even to the nudges of our Father's voice. We remain a bound corpse.

In the mummy game, breaking free from the toilet paper is easy. However, breaking free from the musty layers of fear can prove to be more of a challenge; that is, if we choose to fight in our strength. Figuratively speaking, allowing the Father to take His shears of redemption and cut us loose from the bondage of fear will set us free. Isaiah 43:1b says, "Fear not, for I have redeemed you; I have called you by your name; You are Mine."

UNBEARABLE CHANGE

The enemy plans to open doors of fear. Once opened, he will run amuck in your mind. Disguised with an appealing allure, with a presentation that many can't resist, he invades your life. Repeatedly, he offers an invitation to a land that seems full of promise and potential, but once you step inside, you see his lies. He sucks you in like a vacuum, tirelessly stripping you of yourself. Once the illusion is presented, he convinces you that you can never be who you once were. You can never go back. You are too broken, too damaged, too trapped under an avalanche of shame—you run and hide from any love.

Clashingly different, the Father opens a door of peace, love, and freedom. Deception is nowhere in Him. Therefore, His door offers perfect rest for every space in our lives. The door He presents offers the reassurance that the "real you" is more than enough.

John 20:19-20 shares the story of Jesus' disciples after His death and the desperate fear in which they found themselves mummified.

> On the evening of that first day of the week, the doors being locked where the disciples were assembled, for fear of the Jews, Jesus came and stood in their midst, and said to them, "Peace be with you." When He had said this, He showed them His hands and His side. The disciples were then glad when they saw the Lord (MEV).

The disciples were experiencing unbearable change after Jesus' death, and they were trying to create a semblance of normalcy as they gathered together. The eye-opening reality of being without Him had undoubtedly left them in shock, heartbroken, and now fearing for their very lives. Having no access to the Lord, it was on them to make decisions; so locking themselves away from the world seemed to be the safest option. Jesus, knowing the plight they were in, showed up, brought peace, and began the process of cutting them free from fear.

Like the disciples, we often choose to lock ourselves in a room of fear, doubt, and disbelief. We question everything in our lives, believing the worst of ourselves and others. Consequently, we hide out in shame. Jesus, though knowing the plight we're in, enters our locked rooms and sets things straight. He clears the room of fear, proclaims peace, and again proves Himself the King.

Here's the thing, even if we don't believe who we are, the door to fear that we have locked will not stop the King from entering. So why lock the door? Why do we insist on fighting against the plan He has for our lives and on surrendering to fear instead of the Father? His love conquers all fear. First John 4:18-19 says, "There is no fear in love; but perfect love casts out fear, because fear involves torment.

But he who fears has not been made perfect in love. We love Him because He first loved us." We are often guilty of acting like a baby fighting sleep, who eventually tires out and gives up the unneeded fight. When we realize our resistance to the Father's peace is foolish, we stop the struggle and rest in calm and peaceful sleep. I wonder if that is how He holds us? He sees the struggle and cradles us through the opposition. All the time He knows that when we let go, peace will be so sweet.

> **Jesus, though knowing the plight we're in, enters our locked rooms and sets things straight.**

While they were still in the locked room, Jesus continued to tell the disciples in John 20:21, "As the Father has sent Me, I also send you." He sent them out to change the world, disregarding their fear, shame, and denial. None of those hindrances altered the plan. He released them from the mental torment they had projected on themselves and perhaps said, despite it all, you are Mine, and you are called. He says the same words to the church today, "As the Father has sent Me, I also send you." Whether the door is locked or not, He will still make an entrance.

The disciples were taking steps in the right direction to becoming fearless. The next time they met together, the door was still shut but not locked. Verse 26 says, "After eight days His disciples were again inside with the doors shut. . . . Jesus came and stood among them, and said, 'Peace be with you'" (MEV). Eight days later, the door was shut, not locked. Their foreboding fear was beginning to dissipate.

I love the symbolism of numbers in the Bible. While I'm no numerical expert, I'm very intrigued by it all. Eight means new beginnings, a new order, or new creation. Jesus knew His disciples were ready for a fresh start and renewed vision. You see, when fear leaves, we are given a fresh slate, opening the door to confidence and closing the door to fear. We begin a journey with the Lord that will far surpass our highest expectations. Ephesians 3:20 says, "Now to Him who is able to do exceedingly abundantly above all that we ask or think, according to the power that works in us." He's waiting on us to unlock the door to fear and move into a dimension of authority and power above all we could ever dream.

A short time later the disciples were out of the closed-off room. They were in public, fishing and back to their old lifestyles. Their walls had crumbled, and progress was being made; however, the power was still missing. Pentecost was close at hand, which would launch them into realms of courage and boldness. In Acts 2:14, Peter, full of power, and fear nowhere in sight, stood with the eleven disciples and boldly preached to the crowds with words that "cut to the heart," and three thousand were saved.

> **"He's waiting on us to unlock the door to fear and move into a dimension of authority and power above all we could ever dream. "**

Fear traps us in a locked room, but boldness and confidence in Christ open doors and destinies that no man or enemy can shut. Revelation 3:7-8 explains,

"These are the words of him who is holy and true, who holds the key of David. What he opens no one can shut, and what he shuts no one can open. I know your deeds. See, I have placed before you an open door that no one can shut. I know that you have little strength, yet you have kept my word and have not denied my name" (NIV).

IMPRESS ME CASEY

I would hardly consider myself even a novice in the world of horses. My experience is limited to my family horse—Impress Me Casey—Casey for short. He was a beautiful quarter horse with a red coat and flaxen mane and tail. We had him only a few years during my childhood. I would listen attentively as my dad explained how to care for him. I remember standing on the picnic table to brush his coat while dad put new shoes on him. I would dream about riding Casey swiftly through the fields with my hair blowing in the wind, but in reality, I rode him only with Dad right beside me, because when it came down to it, he terrified me.

Dad taught himself many things about horses during that season of life, one being that tunnel vision is particularly important for them to stay on track. Blinders prevent horses from seeing what is beside or beyond them during a race, enabling their eyes to focus on the prize. This is a fact that I tend to believe is highly important for our battle with fear. Hebrews 12:2 reinforces this, "Keep your eyes on Jesus, who both began and finished this race we're in. Study how he did it. Because he never lost sight of where he was headed—that exhilarating finish in and with God" (MSG). Once you start looking to the right or left, you will find Satan taunting and tormenting you with fear. Any distraction that will stifle our spiritual gifts and create fear, he will not hesitate to push into our line of sight.

Our enemy has mastered the use of illusion to plague God's people with twisted images, creating chaos and confusion. We frequently play into his hand by allowing our imaginations to go wild. His mirage of lies used against us to blur vision and distort beliefs has indeed won him victories. That being said, when we realize who is attacking, we can boldly counter-attack, install fear in our foe, and march in victory. The enemy means to promote our demise, but his plans fail when our eyes are indeed opened, and we see the fight belongs to the Lord. We see this in action in 2 Kings 6:16-17:

> So he answered, "Do not fear, for those who are with us are more than those who are with them." And Elisha prayed, and said, "LORD, I pray, open his eyes that he may see." Then the LORD opened the eyes of the young man, and he saw. And behold, the mountain was full of horses and chariots of fire all around Elisha.

Now is the time for the Lord to open our eyes as He did for Elisha's servant, allowing us to see our adversary as He sees him. Satan wants to restrict our sight, pushing us to hone in on the negative and negate any chance for victory. On the contrary, our Father longs to give us tunnel vision, giving us sight that produces success. Elisha's servant couldn't visualize the truth, and fear ruled supreme until his eyes were miraculously opened. Likewise, our eyes require supernatural blinders, omitting the lies of the enemy and equipping us with heavenly tunnel vision.

Tunnel vision, or loss of peripheral vision, can bring a feeling of claustrophobia. However, tunnel vision, as it concerns the Lord, accomplishes the exact opposite effect.

> **"** *The enemy means to promote our demise, but his plans fail when our eyes are indeed opened, and we see the fight belongs to the Lord.* **"**

It opens a world of spiritual sight, that elicits life-altering moments with the Father, permits a glimpse into the supernatural, and allows you to see what only He wants in your line of sight. Essentially, tunnel vision keeps you on course, assures a victory, and prevents you from falling to the distractions of the enemy.

BRAVE? YES!

Growing up, our daughter, Lexi, was allowed to express her personality by decorating her bedroom door however she wanted—it was the entranceway into her domain. Her door represented the end of the rest of the family's territory and the beginning of her world. And she wanted it to captivate your attention! She wanted it to show her personality and scream, "Lexi Bailey lives here!" This child of mine is the best at seizing every moment and is the epitome of fun. At a young age, she began working on her bucket list and was bound and determined to mark off each item. A natural-born risk-taker, like her father, she would never let fear stop her. On the top of her list was skydiving. I barely conquered my fear of a Ferris wheel! There is no way in a million years I would jump out of a perfectly good airplane, but she decided she was going to jump. After her eighteenth birthday, we loaded up the car and drove her and a friend to South Georgia on a mission. Despite my best efforts to discourage her, my dare-devil child was determined. She seized her moment, took a leap of faith, and jumped 13,500 feet out of a plane.

I do not believe anyone or anything could ever convince me to gear up, board a plane, and jump. Nonetheless, the thought seems invigorating and exhilarating in my imagination, but not in my reality. I will keep it at that, just a hypothetical daydream, not dissimilar to riding through the flowery fields on Casey. So often we want to take a leap of faith and soar, but even a modicum of fear can bring us to a standstill. The closer we get to the edge, the faster our hearts beat. The nagging feeling of dread overcomes us, and we back down. Can you imagine what would happen if the fear of falling did not fester in our emotions? All the energy we exert on precautions and safeguarding against our fears disappears and can be redirected toward the jump we long to make.

" *Our emotions are God-given, however, and if not guarded closely, they can stall and hinder our calling.* **"**

Fighting to keep our feelings in balance is no joke. Feelings can and will fail us, raging war by coercing us into believing the lies of our enemy. Allowing ourselves to settle for fear brings a crippling effect of regret and sorrow. Our feelings do not disqualify us from service. Our emotions are God-given, however, and if not guarded closely, they can stall and hinder our calling. I love this Nelson Mandela quote:

"I learned that courage was not the absence of fear,
but the triumph over it.

The brave man is not he who does not feel afraid,
but he who conquers that fear."

Bravely giving the Lord our yes will transform the dynamics of our lives.

While living in Birmingham, Alabama, I was given a bad report from the doctor. Our ministry team was preparing to leave for a week-long missions trip in a few days. Pulling myself together and keeping my feelings at bay had to happen, and quickly. The news I received was from the enemy to install confusion, fear, and questioning. However, pushing through with the trip was necessary, and determining in my heart to bravely say yes to God's plan and no to fear had to permeate my mind. I had no choice but to trust God and believe the report was incorrect. After returning, we were all changed. God had moved and allowed our team to experience His glory. Praise God, my doctor's report also had changed. In the face of fear, I pushed through the door of doubt, gave the Lord my yes, and took my leap of faith. He, of course, was faithful!

DOOR OF FAITH

Indisputable success over fear comes when you have conquered the voice of self-destruction in your mind. It is the voice that continually brings accusations against your belief and worth in Christ. That voice perpetuates lies and despair. Refuse to believe his words, and reach for what the Father has waiting for you. Whether He opens a door or closes a door, we must trust and turn from our fear. We must accept that a closed door is sometimes needed to keep out disbelief and to create an environment for the supernatural.

Much can be accomplished behind God's closed doors, and the Bible gives us two wonderful examples of just that. In 2 Kings 4:4, we read of a closed door giving one last glimpse of hope to a widow in need, "And when you have come in, you shall shut the door behind you and your sons; then pour it [oil] into all those vessels, and set aside the full ones." Oil was poured behind closed doors, and she and her sons were saved from their enemy. Provision was given to this little family, removing all fear and restoring an optimistic hope for the future. The second example is found in 2 Kings 4:32-33. It says, "When Elisha came into the house, he saw the child lying dead on his bed. So he went in and shut the door behind the two of them and prayed to the LORD" (ESV). The prophet went behind a closed door, prayed, and the Father met him, bringing the dead back to life.

> **"** *Whether He opens a door or closes a door, we must trust and turn from our fear.* **"**

Doors are important. They lead to places of anointing, healing, and beautiful rewards for His children. Matthew 6:6 says, "But you, when you pray, go into your room, and when you have shut your door, pray to your Father who is in the secret place; and your Father who sees in secret will reward you openly." Let me emphasize again, our Father will open some doors of faith and some He will close. What is of paramount importance is to remember He has a plan, and it is without exception, trustworthy.

What door of faith is waiting for you? Perhaps it's time to, with a glimmer of clarity and unmistakable courage, break free from your musty layers of fear and open the door the Father has prepared for your life. It will take courage, risky faith, and absence of fear to enter the door. What is on the other side is a mystery; however, knowing He created the door of faith forces your fear to flee. Moving the boulder of fear and reaching out for the doorknob takes courage. The enemy will do anything to stop you from walking through the door. He and his cohorts use any means available to slap your hand off the knob and detour you from walking through the door. Rest assured, God prepared the door, and once you're there, faith will rise. You've come this far, so why not? Allow the Father to free you from fear. Turn the knob, and push open the door, because revelation awaits.

The fear of man brings a snare, but whoever puts his trust in the LORD will be safe
(Proverbs 29:25 MEV).

7
Trust When Wounded

He is not afraid of bad news; his heart is firm,
*trusting in the L*ORD
(Psalm 112:7 ESV).

My Aunt Rose had been the "mean woman" who, from my perspective, had stolen away my favorite uncle. My seven-year-old heart had developed a strong degree of selfishness and callousness toward my new aunt, knowing full well she could not love my uncle as much as I did. We could never be friends. When the couple announced that they would be serving the Church of God Ministry to the Military in Germany, I felt as though I would never see my uncle again. I believed the newlyweds' decision to move away was completely her fault. I was forced to wipe the tears from my eyes to bid the pair farewell. However, as time passed, her kindness, sweet spirit, and gentle good-bye hugs melted my heart, and I began thinking, "Maybe she's not so bad." Her approval rating continued to rise with the gummy bears and chocolates she would bring home from Germany, making any kid learn to appreciate the relationship.

Being raised Catholic had instilled in her a high regard for the Pope, and she and her mother had planned a trip to see him. This day was of utmost importance to Rose, so she pushed through many obstacles and multiple roadblocks the Lord had put in her path. She was bound and determined to move forward. Wednesday, May 13, 1981, finally arrived, and she and her mother found themselves in St. Petersburg Square, cheering with the crowds of people.

Shortly afterward, my family sat at the kitchen table, watching the news on a 12-inch, portable, black and white TV. There had been an assassination attempt on Pope John Paul II's life, and the world was watching. The news anchors also reported that two women had been caught in the crossfire, one being a Rose Hill. We knew Aunt Rose was there, but there was no way that could be her. After all, the last name was Hall, not Hill. I remember laying my head on the kitchen table and praying, "God, please don't let it be her. I'm sorry I didn't like her at first. Please don't let it be my Aunt Rose." After what seemed like an eternity, the phone rang, and Dad, in the process of calming everyone down, stopped to answer the call. The news was incorrect. It was indeed Rose Hall, and we were given little information other than she was alive and to pray. Tears streamed down my face as I prayed more intensely than I ever had up until that point, and this time around, my selfish motives had vanished.

The ramifications of my aunt's trip were more costly than she could have imagined. One of the four bullets to hit the Pope went through his left index finger, into Rose's elbow, and into the chest of the woman behind her. Her elbow was shattered by the bullet, leaving her in excruciating pain. If she had known upfront the agony she would have to endure, she never would have made the journey. The pain was too intense, and the wound was too severe. However, not only did she see the Pope, but she also met him and stood by his hospital bedside. He prayed for the two wounded women, and Rose is in the history books today. As a side note, she is now one of my closest friends and prayer partners.

> **"** *Dreams can go terribly wrong, and, by all appearances, be completely derailed, but the Father uses the journey.* **"**

We sometimes experience wounds because we refuse to listen to the voice of our Father when He sends warnings. Sometimes they come at the hands of others, and other wounds come at the hands of the enemy. We are wounded and left feeling regret, even still the Father stays by our side. He never abandons His children, and He uses every hardship for His glory. We are assured in Romans 8:28, "So we are convinced that every detail of our lives is continually woven together for good, for we are his lovers who have been called to fulfill his designed purpose" (TPT).

Life rarely turns out how you expect. Dreams can go terribly wrong, and, by all appearances, be completely derailed, but the Father uses the journey. Rose got closer to the Pope than anyone, but if she had understood from the Lord's initial roadblocks what was about to happen, she would have passed. At the least, she would have been fine staying hidden in the crowd and seeing him from a distance. But with a wave of love, God looks at the journey we created, and He reaches out for His wounded children.

OUR SAFE PLACE

I was grocery shopping when I received the call from my daughter's cheerleading coach saying, "Lexi has hurt her leg and you might want to have it looked at, but I doubt there's much wrong. She hasn't even cried." She was wounded but kept a strong front until she saw me, and then the tears flowed. Her safe place arrived, and she could then break and be real. Stopping the tough-girl facade and allowing her pain to show, she held tightly to my neck. She had indeed been injured, twisting her leg and severely breaking it in three places.

Oftentimes, we stoically force our pain from showing in the crowds, but inside we are longing for our safe place. With our Father's embrace, we are allowed to freely express every emotion, every feeling, every heartbreak. We can trust Him with our wounds and our pains, whether they are self-inflicted or by someone else's hand, knowing that either way, He is reaching out with compassion and love.

When we focus on our circumstances instead of the face of our Father, we feel like throwing in the towel. Our physical senses are in control, leaving our spiritual senses as an afterthought. Only allowing ourselves to see what is right before our eyes and not the promises of God, creates a space for depression and loneliness. Our emotional pendulum swings, producing unprecedented heartbreak that consumes our sight, hearing, touch, smell, and taste. Food becomes bland, colors are gray, touch feels forced, the scent is nonexistent, and sounds are muffled by sadness. This is exactly what Psalm 115:4-11 says about trusting our idols instead of our Father:

> Their idols are silver and gold, the work of men's hands. They have mouths, but they cannot speak; eyes, but they cannot see; they have

ears, but they cannot hear; noses, but they cannot smell; they have hands, but they cannot feel; feet, but they cannot walk; neither can they speak with their throat. Those who make them are like them; so is everyone who trusts in them. O Israel, trust in the LORD; He is their help and their shield. O house of Aaron, trust in the LORD; He is their help and their shield. You who fear the LORD, trust in the LORD; He is their help and their shield (MEV).

Idols of self-reliance become an exaggerated imitation of safety, wounding our ability to see the Father as our supreme safe place.

> **"** *We can trust Him with our wounds and our pains, whether they are self-inflicted or by someone else's hand, knowing that either way, He is reaching out with compassion and love.* **"**

In contrast, when we run to Him, we still recognize the grief, but His presence changes our viewpoint. We are no longer calloused, colors are vibrant, tastes are refreshing, and aromas are pleasant. We can hear past the drama and connect to His promises, welcoming His warm embrace amid our pain. Having a wishy-washy, muddled-down version of joy does not have to be our reality when He is our rock and our safe place. Isaiah 26:3-4 says, "You will keep him in perfect peace, whose mind is stayed on You, because he trusts in You. Trust in the LORD forever, for in GOD the LORD we have an everlasting rock" (MEV).

> **"** *Idols of self-reliance become an exaggerated imitation of safety, wounding our ability to see the Father as our supreme safe place.* **"**

Relationships with complete trust yield an emotional place of safety. My husband says, "If I say there's cheese on the mountain, put crackers in your backpack." Though I used to laugh at his playful arrogance, over the years our relationship has deepened, and I now 100 percent believe there's cheese. He says it. I believe it. I trust him; therefore, I will respond without hesitation. Accepting the Father as our safe place permits us to drop our barriers and experience perfect peace. When trust of this magnitude exists, we come to a place of rest beyond human understanding. This is a trust that is built on proven behavior, not on feelings or emotions. This is a place where worry melts away, struggles diminish, and anxiety is nowhere to be found. Peace does not mean we do not have storms; it means we have Jesus.

SOMEONE ELSE'S FAULT

In a perfect world, suffering undeservingly would be unknown; unfortunately, it is more rampant than we would want to admit. Second Samuel 4:4 tells the story of a young boy who faced undeserved pain at the hand of another, leaving him injured for life. "Saul's son Jonathan had a son named Mephibosheth, who had not been able to walk since he was five years old. It happened when someone from Jezreel told his nurse that Saul and Jonathan had died. She hurried off with the boy in her arms, but he fell and injured his legs" (CEV). This innocent little guy was born to the son of the king, royalty, and now he was wounded when someone else dropped him. As a result of that mistake, Mephibosheth recedes into the background, no longer operating in his right as a royal prince.

Maybe that's your story. Someone else wounded/abused you. It wasn't your fault, and yet you have taken on that shame. You were the victim. Someone else's failures make you feel like you cannot even walk! Wounds that come from others' mistakes or sins can be particularly disruptive, and deep healing is required from our Father. Psalm 34:18 reminds us, "The LORD is near the brokenhearted; he saves those crushed in spirit" (CSB).

" *Peace does not mean we do not have storms; it means we have Jesus.* **"**

The message of Mephibosheth ends with a restoration as God dispels every ounce of shame, and Mephibosheth reclaims his invitation to the king's table! You too are royalty, a child of the most high King, deserving of healing, grace, and restoration.

BROKEN POTTERY

In the Book of Job, we witness disaster heaped upon disaster. Job's life is in shambles, and he is left alone with no one to comfort him when he reaches for a broken piece of pottery. Job 2:8-9 reads, "Then Job sat on the ash-heap to show his sorrow. And while he was scraping his sores with a broken piece of pottery, his wife asked, 'Why do you still trust God? Why don't you curse him and die?'" (CEV).

Job took brokenness and used it to bring healing, scraping pain off himself, and soothing his wounds. From the perspective of the pottery, its existence was over. Tragedy in some form had caused its demise, rendering it useless. This potsherd found itself thrown out with the trash, leaving it feeling damaged and worthless, but in God's sovereign plan its brokenness helped bring healing to someone else.

What if in the process of trusting the Father with your brokenness, God could use you to help soothe the hurting and the pain of someone else? Will you trust the Father to use your pain? Second Corinthians. 4:8-9 says, "We are hard-pressed on every side, yet not crushed; we are perplexed, but not in despair; persecuted, but not forsaken; struck down, but not destroyed." Our Father restores the angry, lonely, betrayed, rejected, scared, and brokenhearted, reminding them they are worthy and can be used as a catalyst for change. He longs for us to use the pain that we endured and the healing we received to help heal others.

PRUNING IS PAINFUL

On leave one weekend, my father, then a United States Army paratrooper, stood at his sweetheart's front door with two dozen red roses, prepared to ask the most important question of his life. Thankfully, my mom said yes, and my parents married one week later. Before moving onto the military base, my mom's Aunt Audine took two of her roses and replanted them in the yard, where they took root, grew, and multiplied. After a few years, two rose bushes stood strong and healthy. My dad has twice moved those now fifty-year-old rose bushes to different homes. Every fall they are pruned back to the stub and the roots, removing all the unwanted dead wood and overgrowth. Consequently, these once beautiful bushes are wounded, stripped bare, and yet this process ensures they will grow back bigger and stronger.

You may be asking the question, what's the difference in being pruned and being wounded? Aren't they the same? I had the same thought process, and although they both involve pain, they are remarkably diffcrent in one major way. Wounds are inflicted by ourselves or by others, whereas pruning comes from the hand of the Father. He takes us through the painful steps of pruning to recapture a more beautiful state, where we are stronger and able to reproduce ourselves.

" *What if in the process of trusting the Father with your brokenness, God could use you to help soothe the hurting and the pain of someone else?* **"**

I am not much of a horticulturist. Until recently, every plant I touched died and quickly. However, when Rob gave me a beautiful plant for Mother's Day, I wanted to keep it living as long as possible. What grabbed my attention was that pruning was a messy process: my hands got dirty; I had cuts from the thorns; my fresh manicure was messed up; and the countertop was covered in a sticky residue. The unruly growth was stopped, but the plant looked a fright, and it took days to clean up all the aftereffects. I never thought about pruning being painful for the owner who has loved and grown the plant. You hate to see the beauty fade, but you know the end product will be worth the steps taken. The plant will return fuller and stronger.

The Father won't allow wild overgrowth, so He must break off the dead and unruly branches in our lives. In John 15:1-2 Jesus says, "I am the true vine, and my Father is the gardener. He cuts away every branch of mine that doesn't produce fruit. But he trims clean every branch that does produce fruit, so that it will produce even more fruit" (CEV). Pruning removes the dead and dying to restore new growth and produce high-quality fruit. Undergoing this process is painful and messy and leaves us feeling bare, exposed, and ugly; however, a beautiful tree cut down by its owner will in time be restored and renewed, becoming more than its original version. First Peter 5:10 says, "And then, after your brief suffering, the God of all loving grace, who has called you to share in his eternal glory in Christ, will personally and powerfully restore you and make you stronger than ever. Yes, he will set you firmly in place and build you up" (TPT).

> **"***He takes us through the painful steps of pruning to recapture a more beautiful state, where we are stronger and able to reproduce ourselves.* **"**

Drawing close to the Lord seems to come easier during pain, pruning, and dark times. Why? In our wounded state, we are more vulnerable and willing to desperately cry out for the help that He alone can provide.

GET UP AND DANCE

His presence was beautiful one day as I worshiped. The song "Rain Dance," by Judy Jacobs, came on my playlist. I hadn't heard that song for some time, but when it began, it felt like part of me. Warfare and worship intercession surged the atmosphere and dance flowed from the deepest part of me. Keep in mind I have almost no dance training, and this dance was definitely unto the Lord. I put the song on repeat and immersed myself in the moment. Over the next several days, the same pattern followed. I was drawn to that song week after week. At that point, I knew the Lord was commissioning me to dance, and this would no doubt continue. Some days I would dance before the Lord for twenty minutes, and some days an hour. Being keenly aware this season was purposeful, I warred against the enemy's camp. Proclaiming the victory I walked in brought about life-changing freedom, and a sense of resolve pumped through my veins. I would not be defeated. For six months, I soared, fully prepared to conquer the world and see the glory of God.

But in one moment, our lives completely changed. A portentous Category 5 whirlwind had smashed into our home and sent us into a wild spiral out of our control. With no conceivable end in sight, I wondered what in the world was happening. I could not comprehend how, within this spiritually high season, the enemy could so fiercely attack.

I was at a dead end, feeling entirely defeated; my dance stopped. For two weeks, I paced back and forth, crying to God. There was no dance, no shout. There were little prayers, but mostly there were tears. On my face before the Lord, I cried out, "This wound is more than I can take, God. I can't even breathe." I fully expected a compassionate response, but what I received was much different. He spoke to my spirit, "Get up and dance for Me." I argued back, "Did you not just hear what I said? I can't breathe, let alone dance." At that moment, I had to decide if I was going to trust Him and obey or lie there on my face. Before my worship had freely flowed, now I was hitting a wall. Reluctantly standing, I cried out to the Lord, "I Trust You!" Wounded, weak, but determined, I turned on "Rain Dance." At first, I could barely move, but as the music soaked into my spirit, my dance returned, and His presence strengthened my weak knees. Supreme calm filled the air, and I could breathe again. I was drinking in His presence like someone dying of thirst from an extended drought. Guzzling His life-sustaining water, I danced before the Lord and announced to the enemy, "You will rue the day you messed with my family." I reminded him that the Father speaks out of whirlwinds, Nahum 1:3 says, "The LORD has His way in the whirlwind and in the storm, and the clouds are the dust of His feet."

I ENTRUSTED MY LIFE

Our heavenly Father has not only watched us, but also He has held us through some of our worst wounds and heartaches. No matter the circumstances, He gently leads us back to a place where we can catch our breath, strengthen our legs, and move forward. We move forward with scars, regrets, and heartaches, but we also move forward stronger, wiser, healed, and more trusting of Him. Eventually, we not only move, but we also dance.

Looking past the pain, believing the truth, and opting to hear the caring, loving words of our Father frees us. Hebrews 12:2 lets us know we are not alone in suffering. Jesus showed us perfect faith when He endured the cross and scorned its shame. He understands wounds that come from others completely. Why? Because He lived it Himself.

He suffered, taking our grief, sins, and sorrows upon Himself, substituting His wounds for ours, in a beautiful demonstration of love. At the cross, He received necessary wounds for us to have redemptive grace and healing. He does not take your pain or suffering lightly, quite the opposite, it grieves Him when His children suffer. In my experience, He cradled me through the heartache.

Deep wounds you try to release but continually resurface must be surrendered to your Father. How can you trust when you are afraid to be vulnerable? Trust requires surrender, and surrender requires relinquishing control, which results in obedience and victory. During His greatest pain, Jesus shouted His complete surrender to His Father, trusting His life into His hands. Luke 23:46 says, "Crying out in a loud voice, Jesus said, 'Father, into your hands I entrust my life.' After he said this, he breathed for the last time" (CEB). Words before His last breath were used to reiterate the importance of surrender and trust. I wonder if that could be your heart's cry today, "Father, into your hands I entrust my life!"

He alone knows the path we will walk. Why wouldn't we trust the only one that can see our journey from beginning to end? In the circumstances we will face that may include pain and are outside our realm of reasoning, He is there. When a logical reason for why doesn't exist, we move

> **"***We move forward with scars, regrets, and heartaches, but we also move forward stronger, wiser, healed, and more trusting of Him.* **"**

forward and trust there's more hope to be found in Him. Through it all, we grow and become more than we could ever envision or rationalize.

My husband and his friends enjoy playing the card game Rook. When a bad hand is dealt their response is, "This is going to be ugly." In all honesty, the hand we are dealt at times is just that—ugly. We have no rational reason for the pain we are facing, and nothing makes sense. These are the moments when our trust and faith in the Father kicks in and brings peace during the storm. Romans 8:28 reinforces that whatever circumstances we find ourselves in, He will turn it around in our favor: "And we know that all things work together for good to those who love God, to those who are the called according to His purpose."

8
Trust Your Differences

I've told you all this so that trusting me,
you will be unshakable and assured,
deeply at peace. In this godless world,
you will continue to experience difficulties.
But take heart! I've conquered the world
(John 16:33 MSG).

Leaf collections are part of most children's elementary education. Researching different trees and the leaves they produce unfolds many lessons. I have fond memories of Dad taking me to visit my great-grandparents' home to gather leaves from their many beautiful fruit trees. My great-grandpa was fascinated with his garden and trees and appreciated the smallest of details and diversity. We walked around their property for hours while Dad and Great-Grandpa educated me on each tree, identifying the leaves, stems, trunks, roots, and what each one produced. If I prodded them for more information and my great-grandpa did not have the answer, he would sidestep the issue, look at my dad and say, "It's just the nature of things. Like Vickie marrying you, Steve." While his response went over my head, Dad patted him on the back and grinned as we moved to the next tree. Once I had a wide variety, we called it a day, but not before we grabbed a drink of warm water from the water hose.

We went through the same process with our son in the fourth grade. We still have that lime-green binder with all the leaves he collected. We compared each leaf, appreciating the beauty and uniqueness, all to know more about each leaf. I love the process of flipping through pages, admiring differences, and exploring the reasons each tree produces such particular variations. My husband often takes walks around our neighborhood with our grandchildren, admiring all the different leaves, and developing their appreciation for nature.

> **"** *Comparison changes the dynamics of the mind and heart; you will find yourself entertaining options which were before unthinkable.* **"**

How easily we value the differences in nature and others, yet we do not have that level of value and appreciation for ourself. Instead, we see our differences as bizarre, defective, or inferior to others. Comparison changes the dynamics of the mind and heart; you will find yourself entertaining options which were before unthinkable. You say, "I would never," and then there you stand in the middle of that unthinkable. You should not feel the need to conform to the lives of others who have no right to influence your standards. Theodore Roosevelt said, "Comparison is the thief of joy." We have all been guilty of comparing ourselves to others. We substitute our uniqueness for a fabricated version of ourselves and have our joy hijacked.

BEAUTIFUL INTERRUPTION

One year into our marriage, Rob and I had rerouted the course we were on when we made a significant decision to move to Cleveland, Tennessce, where he could finish his education at what was then Lee College. At the time, we were living in Maryville, Tennessee, serving as youth pastors at Topside Church of God.

I was working as a dental assistant, not because it was my dream job, but because it was an unexpected opportunity that I surprisingly enjoyed. The work was intriguing, my coworkers became friends, and I loved being around new people throughout the day. Rob was a successful car salesman. This was not his dream job either, but his charismatic personality allowed him to excel and provide for our family until God opened doors in full-time ministry. We were happy, but we knew he needed to finish his college degree. Before we went any further with this move, I needed to check on one crucial thing that could bring a screeching halt to our new plan.

I say new because it was not our first plan. This new scenario had played out after having a realistic discussion about life, goals, and what we should be accomplishing. One month earlier, we looked at each other and said, "Wouldn't a Bailey baby be adorable?" However, that day, we came to our senses and realized we might be too young for parenthood and should check off at least a handful of things from our to-do list before taking on that unexplored adventure. Before reapplying to Lee, however, I felt a quick trip to the local Walgreens might be in our best interests, just to "make sure."

Consequently, we went back to our first plan, bought Grandma and Grandpa coffee mugs, and jumped in the car to visit our parents. I thank God for that beautiful interruption in our lives. Victoria Constance Bailey was born; we were parents, ready or not. Finishing his education later would have to do.

YOU FIX PEOPLE

Setting up Victoria's nursery in our quaint little two-bedroom mobile home was my priority. Finally deciding on the primary colors that would perfectly match her Baby Minnie and Mickey Mouse bedding brought a feeling of accomplishment. I was ready to finish decorating her nursery, and the crib was the only thing missing. Rob and I excitedly got in our silver Oldsmobile and went to Walmart. Less than $100 purchased the infamous Jenny Lind crib.

As we returned home with the crib, Rob filled me in on his intentions to do this project alone. I argued that I was an excellent assistant, but he was on a mission. If he were going to impress me, he thought he had to become my new "Mister fix-it." I was oblivious to the comparison that was tormenting his mind.

As he locked the door to the nursery behind him, Rob said, "I will finish soon, then we can celebrate by going out for dinner." After all, how tough could it be to put a crib together? Neither of us noticed that the job called for two people, nor did we realize the recommended time to complete the project was three to four hours. Every hour or so, I would knock on the door and ask if it was almost ready. We needed to leave for dinner! As each hour passed, my patience grew thinner, and his replies grew gruffer. Rob was certain that my dad could have put that crib together with his eyes closed, and he did not want to admit he was struggling.

After many hours, my strong Marine emerged, proud of his accomplishment, even though there were leftover pieces, and we were both hungry for dinner. Entering the room, I responded with excitement; however, seeing the extra parts gave me pause. Assessing the situation, I began questioning the security and safety of his work. Comparison, unknown to me, had sunk its claws into my husband. Several days later, Rob had my dad give his approval of the crib to put my mind at ease. The structure was fine, but Dad quickly picked up on my husband's uneasiness when Rob said, "I'm not quite the 'fixer' that you are, Steve." My dad's reply was brilliant. He said, "I fix things, Son; you fix people." What a calming and reassuring statement that was, and it helped reframe Rob's thought process. While striving to attain what he perceived as success, my dad opened a space for a different point of view and bolstered Rob's confidence.

This crib lasted almost ten years and held our four most precious possessions. Despite the frustrating beginning and the missing parts, the crib made it through. This statement holds true for most of life's adventures. We both had plenty of learning ahead of us, and the "Bailey crib" was only the beginning.

“ *The Lord longs for our relationship with Him to be comfortable, where we can be true to ourselves, our strengths, and our weaknesses.* **”**

Becoming content and comfortable together, even in the middle of a mess, and surrounded by broken and extra pieces, is a sign of a trusting relationship. Rob and I recently put together bunkbeds for our grandbabies. These treehouse bunkbeds were so much more complex than anything we have put together in our twenty-eight years of marriage. However, building it was an endeavor filled with such laughter and wonderful memories. Evident in the speed and precision of the construction, I saw that my strong Marine had become much better with tools in his forties than he was as a young man! After a few hours of laughter, a gallon of coffee, and a good bit of flirting, we both emerged proud of *our* accomplishment. We are proud to say that the bunk beds were finished with no extra parts!

The Lord longs for our relationship with Him to be comfortable, where we can be true to ourselves, our strengths, and our weaknesses. He wants us to be able to laugh, work, and accomplish goals with Him. When He is present, differences seem insignificant, and He never makes us feel belittled. He gives us the personal freedom to relax, let go, trust, and go for the ride. Seeing ourselves from His particular vantage point aligns our trajectory with greatness, and allows comparison to melt away.

WHOSE APPROVAL DO YOU SEEK?

Comparison promotes pride, and it pressures you to become keenly aware of traits or abilities in others that are meaningless in your journey. This pressure grows swiftly and transforms into the green-eyed monster of jealousy and envy. Because of sin, God's people began comparing themselves to the other nations and desiring what they had.

First Samuel 8:1-5 tells the story of sin that led to comparison, and the result altered lives and nations.

> And it came about when Samuel was old, that he installed his sons as judges for Israel. Now the name of his firstborn son was Joel, and the name of his second son was Abijah. They were

judging in Beersheba. But his sons did not walk in his way, for they followed after unlawful gain, and they took bribes, and they perverted justice. And all the elders of Israel gathered together and they came to Samuel at Ramah. They said to him, "You are old and your sons do not walk in your ways. Now, install for us a king to govern us like all the nations" (MEV).

The prophet Samuel's two sons' bribery and dishonest dealings opened the door for doubt among the people of God, and they became unhappy with their leadership. Rightfully so! The sons' decision to do what was best for themselves instead of what was best for the people resulted in a betrayal of God. Perhaps comparisons made by the people resulted in a lack of confidence, but the opposite was true for the sons, and they became entitled and arrogant. Satan is all about adulations and egos that create a self-absorbed attitude which, in turn, destroys. He has no problem lifting you up, knowing the higher you rise, the farther you will fall and the more people you will affect.

❝ *Betrayals will come, and people will fail you, but be cautious to stop the comparison cycle that creates a rift in the plans the Father has in motion for your life.* **❞**

It was not merely that the Israelites wanted to be like other nations, but they witnessed dirty leadership, which got them thinking. You see, bad leadership turned hearts away from God, and thought processes moved to, "The grass is greener on the other side." "We want to be like other nations, ruled by a human king." Betrayals will come, and people will fail you, but be cautious to stop the comparison cycle that creates a rift in the plans the Father has in motion for your life. Because of the comparisons, God was ousted as the king of Israel. The enemy wants nothing more than for you, too, to lose trust in your Father and switch leadership, leaving you controlled by man and his opinion of you. I love how Galatians 1:10 puts it, **"For am I now seeking the approval of man, or of God? Or am I trying to please man? If I were still trying to please man, I would not be a servant of Christ"** (ESV). What wonderful questions for self-evaluation! Whose approval are you seeking? Are you wanting to blend in until there is nothing unique left of who God has made you? Of course not, therefore, pushing aside the opinions and approval of others is instrumental in an upward climb with the Father.

STOP ARGUING AND GO

When you move forward and trust that you are the exact servant Christ made you to be, the scrutiny of others becomes meaningless in your life and actions. The truth is no one has the right to dictate who you are, other than your heavenly Father. Let His words concerning you be what you believe and stand on. He defines you and pushes you to greater belief in who you are in Him. He desires to reverse your mindset and redirect your self-image to reflect Him in you. You must be on board with His plan and fix your eyes upon His gaze.

He will not allow what you are doing currently to sidetrack your destiny, but will you? Amos 7:14-15 says, "But Amos answered Amaziah: 'I am no prophet, and I am no prophet's disciple. Rather, I am a herdsman and a dresser of sycamore trees.' But the LORD took me away from the flock, and the LORD said to me, 'Go, prophesy to My people Israel'" (MEV). Amos protested that he was not a prophet in any shape or form, and that fact had zero bearing on God's plan for him to prophesy. Arguing the call, with all the reasons he was unqualified, sounds way too familiar. Making lists of why someone else is the more obvious choice or why what you offer is flawed and grossly inadequate, is an easy trap in which to fall. And without hesitation, comparison pounces on your self-image, belittling any shred of confidence you possess.

"Go" was the response given by the Father. No coddling or pampering, simply do what I say. Stop with the excuses and go. Your abilities and giftings will adapt to His desire. When you step out in faith, He gives you what you need to fulfill His plan. Square your shoulders, set your heart on the prize, and go for it.

Trust His eye to guide you because what He sees in you is what matters. Amos was an ordinary man going about life in a normal fashion, yet despite his commonplace and average lifestyle, God had a purpose. Amos's lack of preparation, training, or job experience was not a consideration to God. See your destiny through the eyes of your Father! This rationale will also allow you to see the enemy's schemes for what they truly are—a last-ditch effort to manipulate and control your emotions. See the truth! Believe the truth!

“ *Trust His eye to guide you because what He sees in you is what matters.* **”**

Our human ideologies are oftentimes warped, making our Father's words appear implausible in our reality. Still, John 16:33 says that you will question things and why they are the way they are. But trusting Him is what makes you unshakable, assured, and deeply at peace.

> *In your doubts, remember that your human wisdom and reasoning rebels against the truth.*

You will question; it is human nature. In your doubts, remember that your human wisdom and reasoning rebels against the truth. Satan wears a false veneer of compassion and empathy, saying, "You are the only one to ever face this." "There's no way you are capable." "Someone else is more qualified." "It's okay to walk away this time." Refuse to listen to his tirade. Trust your Father, and be free from the disturbance and demoralization of the enemy. John assures that trusting the Father brings unwavering confidence and peace. You do not have to feel capable within yourself; just completely trust Him. Psalm 32:8-9 says,

> I hear the Lord saying, "I will stay close to you, instructing and guiding you along the pathway for your life. I will advise you along the way and lead you forth with my eyes as your guide. So don't make it difficult; don't be stubborn when I take you where you've not been before. Don't make me tug you and pull you along. Just come with me!" (TPT)

9

Trust During Warfare

Many of them are pursuing and attacking me,
but even when I am afraid,
I keep on trusting you
(Psalm 56:2-3 CEV).

Two nights a week, after dinner, I would pass the parenting baton to Rob, and he would take over the nighttime rituals with the children. A few weeks prior, I had overheard our office was looking for someone to come after hours and clean the facilities. Seeing this as my opportunity for some much needed personal time, I jumped at the chance. This new regimen had become our normal routine, and I thoroughly enjoyed the silence and solitude it offered. Being a welcomed break from reality, it was a time I could spend thinking about anything I wanted, without interruption. It was relaxing and helped me be a better mommy. Surprisingly, cleaning an office became my enjoyable "me time."

After quickly straightening up from our spaghetti dinner, I kissed Rob on the cheek and headed toward the office. Vacuuming the last room and almost finished for the night, I was stopped in my tracts when I heard someone beating loudly on the front door. My heart was pounding as I jumped with fear; all I could do was pray for courage to see who was at the door. Initially, when I saw it was Rob, I was upset with him, thinking he was playing a joke on me, trying to be funny. After letting him in, I quickly realized it was no joke. He held me tight saying, "Thank God, you're okay." Still clueless as to what he was referring to, he began to tell me the story from his perspective. "I had gotten the children to bed and sat down to relax and watch television; when I heard the Holy Spirit say, "Go get your wife!" I jumped up and got here as quickly as I could. When I pulled into the parking lot, a man dressed in all black was hiding behind the bushes watching and waiting for you." Rob chased him into the darkness before finally circling back around to the office. A sigh of relief was in his voice, and we were both jolted by the reality of what could have been.

> **" We can't be effective warriors if our heads are in the sand, refusing to admit there is a fight. "**

While enjoying my alone time that night, unknown to me, I had an enemy waiting to pounce. An imminent danger was lurking right outside only a few feet from me, and thankfully my husband listened to the voice of the Father. I am so grateful for the protection of my husband and my God! Time after time, He made certain He was just that—my protector. Second Samuel 22:3 says, "The God of my strength, in whom I will trust; My shield and the horn of my salvation, my stronghold and my refuge; My Savior, You save me from violence."

The man Rob chased away was aware of his plan to harm me, but I wasn't. There was a fight brewing, but I was clueless. In the same way, our enemy is fully aware of the war he is masterminding, but are we? This truth is important information, not to scare us but to remind us of the facts. We can't be effective warriors if our heads are in the sand, refusing to admit there is a fight. First Peter 5:8 says we must be alert, "Be on your guard and stay awake. Your enemy, the devil, is like a roaring lion, sneaking around to find someone to attack" (CEV).

THE ENEMY'S FEAR

Gideon had to hear the voice of the enemy to trust God. God told him he would win, but it took the enemy's dream and fear to convince him. Judges 7:9-11, 13-15 says,

> It happened on the same night that the LORD said to him, "Arise, go down against the camp, for I have delivered it into your hand. But if you are afraid to go down, go down to the camp with Purah your servant, and you shall hear what they say; and afterward your hands shall be strengthened to go down against the camp. . . . And when Gideon had come, there was a man telling a dream to his companion. He said, "I have had a dream: To my surprise, a loaf of barley bread tumbled into the camp of Midian; it came to a tent and struck it so that it fell and overturned, and the tent collapsed." Then his companion answered and said, "This is nothing else but the sword of Gideon the son of Joash, a man of Israel! Into his hand God has delivered Midian and the whole camp." And so it was, when Gideon heard the telling of the dream and its interpretation, that he worshiped. He returned to the camp of Israel, and said, "Arise, for the LORD has delivered the camp of Midian into your hand."

Immediately after hearing the men's conversation, he worshiped, returned to the camp, and said, "Let's go." The enemy's fear activated his faith and leadership. Once he was able to accept who he was, his life and the lives of the people around him changed. Hearing the fear of the enemy propelled him to fight and enabled his ability to believe in himself and the words of the Lord to him.

Rahab expressed the fear of the people toward the Israelites in Joshua 2:8-11.

> Now before they lay down, she came up to them on the roof, and said to the men: "I know that the LORD has given you the land, that the terror of you has fallen on us, and that all the inhabitants of the land are fainthearted because of you. For we have heard how the LORD dried up the water of the Red Sea for you when you came out of Egypt, and what you did to the two kings of the Amorites who were on the other side of the Jordan, Sihon and Og, whom you utterly destroyed. And as soon as we heard these things, our hearts melted; neither did there remain any more courage in anyone because of you, for the LORD your God, He is God in heaven above and on earth beneath."

After Rahab revealed what the people were saying to Joshua's men, they were encouraged, revved up, and ready for war. In verse 24, with assurance, they reported back to Joshua, "Truly the LORD has delivered all the land into our hands, for indeed all the inhabitants of the country are fainthearted because of us." The enemy's fear awakened the boldness of the called. On one rare moment, the Father allowed me to see the fear of my enemy in a dream. Boy, did it hit a nerve and rattle my prayer life. Righteous indignation rose in my soul, readying me for warfare.

FIGHTING FOR LEGACY

Typically, when the Lord speaks to me through a dream, it is either prophetic or revealing in nature, so I strategically know how to pray against the plan of Satan. I have learned over the years, with much training from my mom, not to be fearful concerning these "warning" dreams. They are designed by God to prepare, equip, and encourage me. They remind me that, without a doubt, He is in control. Ephesians 5:13 says, "All things are exposed when they are revealed by the light" (MEV). In this dream, the Lord exposed the plans of the enemy and, as unsettling as it was, it spurred me on toward intercession like no other dream I have ever been given before.

In the dream, I entered through the back doors of a vast assembly hall. Children and teenagers were scattered throughout the hundreds of seats, as more were making their way into the room. I felt unrest as I entered, and the farther I walked in the more the feeling of unrest changed to staggering grief in my spirit. The students already seated were in a locked gaze with the giant screens on either side of the stage. I recognized a few students, who were all mesmerized and unresponsive, as I approached and tried to interact with them. I began walking between the aisles and chairs, realizing not one single adult was in the area. At this point, the Lord allowed me to feel the evil spirit at work. He revealed to me, with blurred, indistinct vision, vile pornographic images transmitting on the screens. I felt an enormous flood of desperation. I yelled, "Why is no one stopping this? Someone, help me!" The feelings of anguish and grief in my heart were indescribable.

Running, desperate to find someone to help me, I noticed a long corridor where women were lined up waiting to use the restroom. As I approached, I knew they were the mothers of the students, but no matter how passionately I yelled, it was as if I didn't exist. "Please, don't you realize what your children are seeing?" I was given no acknowledgment or response. In a state of bewilderment, I ran into the crowded restroom. I watched in amazement as they fixed their makeup, brushed their hair, and talked among themselves as if nothing were wrong. I ran back to the main auditorium waving my arms and screaming for the students to look away from the perversion, but they appeared to be stone statues. Helplessly, I ran back to the restroom again, still with no success.

Out of breath, I prayed, "God show me what to do." He led me down the corridor where I saw an enormous office space. The walls were all glass, allowing me to see the magnitude of the operation. I could see cubicles, for what seemed like miles, that were filled with employees working feverously at their computers. As I entered the glass doors, the receptionist greeted me with a smile. It was apparent the management was made up of well-trained professionals. The operation was impressive, and I was blown away at the diligence and intensity of the employees. Sadly, I knew I would get no help here; they were my opposition, working against my efforts. Terminating this system would not be an easy task, and my spirit was in constant prayer. As I approached the receptionist's desk, her smile changed to a snarl. I demanded, "I need to speak to the manager, now!" Speaking to someone on her headset, she stared me down with a look of utter disdain.

Through one of the glass doors, a tall, thin, well-dressed female walked toward me. Her smile made my stomach turn, and I prayed for courage. Emphatically, I explained to her that the images on the screens must be turned off and that the children in that room did not belong to her. Her sickening smile made me cringe, as she clarified the way this was going to work. "The children are old enough to see the footage we make available, and the parents will not stop us." With boldness I've never experienced before, I moved uncomfortably close to her, put my finger in her face, and said, "I will destroy you!" The pride on her smug face quickly transformed into almost palpable fear. As I awoke from the dream, I asked the Lord, "What was that about?" He responded, "Pray against the spirit of Pan."

HE WANTS OUR CHILDREN

God allowed me to witness an organized, modern-day hub for the enemy's behind-the-scenes-infrastructure, and His instructions to me were to pray against the spirit of Pan. I knew of this spirit from Matthew 16 where Jesus took His disciples to Caesarea Philippi. While standing over the cave of Pan, He asked, "Who do men say that I am?" I had never delved into the subject much deeper, and knowing a better understanding was needed, I jumped right in.

Fairly quickly into my research, I discovered that this half-man, half-goat god is a trickster that leads the young down the wrong path. There are several words used to depict Pan, god of the woods—panic, brings uncontrollable fear that causes irrational behavior, out of control, perverse lying, great musicians, sexual perversion, destruction of marriages, etc. The list goes on and on. It did not take much research to recognize this spirit was after our children, and the dream had painted a clear picture of his dangers.

Sadly, the mothers in the dream were preoccupied with themselves and didn't notice what was taking place right under their noses. Not only was the enemy leading the children astray, but the mothers were lulled into false contentment and spiritual dullness. We must pray to the Father for self-aware-ness that opens our eyes to our own need for revival and leads to clear directives on how to go forward in battle. I can say shortly after the dream, the onslaught of the enemy bombarded our family's doors in full force. My dream didn't stop the attack, but it allowed me to pull my head out of the sand and gear up for battle. Seeing the truth of my complacencies, as difficult as it was to swallow, brought gravity to the warnings of my Father.

In this present day, the spirit of Pan is still rampant in our society and feverishly attacking our youth. There is even a sexual orientation that honors this spirit. There is a direct assault against our children, and it is far too easy to be distracted and caught off guard. It is time to seek God and intercede like never before. The fight is on, and this prophetic dream was the push I needed to engage and partner with the Father in warfare. Ephesians 6:12 explains the fight this way, "We are not fighting against humans. We are fighting against forces and authorities and against rulers of darkness and powers in the spiritual world" (CEV).

The Pan dream showed me the enemy's strategies, and it showed his fear of a Holy Spirit-filled warrior. I was compelled into intercession and warfare for our children with a capacity unlike I had ever experienced before or since. How dare he have the audacity to steal, kill, and destroy the offspring of the Father! Genesis 3:1 tells us the enemy is very subtle in his temptations. The word *subtle*, according to *Strong's Concordance*, means "shrewd, sly, and crafty," and that he may be; however, Isaiah 42:13 says, "The Lord will go forth like a warrior, He will arouse His zeal like a man of war. He will utter a shout, yes, He will raise a war cry. He will prevail against His enemies" (NASB 1995). Our God is partnering with us in this war, awakening us from the humdrum of daily life, and fitting us for battle.

While writing this, our family is mulling around the house trying their best to be active and productive, but still, we are all bored to tears. Why? Because the world is in pandemonium. Fear, confusion, anxiety, and panic are overtaking our society. People are stockpiling water, toilet paper, and cleaning supplies due to the COVID-19 virus.

The enemy is desperately trying to impede our Kingdom knowledge and cloud our spiritual vision of his tactics, and he appears to be making headway. This is none other than the spirit of Pan haunting our world and working feverishly toward setting our eyes on the images playing out before us. His crew is producing one of the greatest pandemics to hit the world this century. It is causing people to be laid off from their jobs, schools to be closed, and people to be asked to stay home.

> "*Our God is partnering with us in this war, awakening us from the humdrum of daily life, and fitting us for battle.*"

The church cannot cower to his threats, remembering the gates of hell will not prevail against the church. I believe the generation Pan was trying to destroy in the dream will be the ones who rise up, fight against his attacks, and bring about revival. We must stay focused on our assignment to intercede on behalf of our children and not allow distraction of any kind to create dullness in our efforts. The enemy quivers in fear when God's people rise against him, and the Father unravels Satan's plans when we pray! Psalm 37:12-13 puts the battle into perspective: "The wicked plots against the just, and gnashes at him with his teeth. The Lord laughs at him, for He sees that his day is coming."

DISTRACTIONS CAN BE DEADLY

I'm reminded of a time when my distraction could have cost my baby's life. Early one morning, we loaded a charter bus full of teenagers, along with our four-year-old daughter and one-year-old son, to attend a youth conference in Mobile, Alabama. Upon arrival, I thoroughly inspected our room for any hazards or potential dangers for my little ones. The sliding glass doors leading to our two-story view of the ocean brought immediate concern. Although the scenery was breathtaking, my heart beat swiftly considering its threat.

The enemy quivers in fear when God's people rise against him, and the Father unravels Satan's plans when we pray!

The children squealed with excitement as they took in the beauty of the ocean. Ensuring their safety, I measured the railings and made sure their heads were too large to fit through, and I removed the small table and chair to stop them from climbing. While doing so, someone knocked on our door, and I quickly brought the children back into the room. Distracted in conversation, and not realizing the sliding glass door was not completely closed, I heard my daughter scream, "Robbie!" I turned to see his little body dangling off the deck. He had put his legs through the railing, squeezed his body through, and was only caught by his head and ear. I have never been so frightened in my life. My body shook for hours as I thought of all the what-ifs.

Learning to Trust the Father's Heart

In retrospect, I should have considered sliding through feet first as a possibility; however, it never crossed my mind. That experience taught me a valuable lesson. Distractions can be deadly.

First Peter 5:8 says, "Keep a cool head. Stay alert. The devil is poised to pounce, and would like nothing better than to catch you napping. Keep your guard up" (MSG). Ignoring the enemy and pretending you're impervious to his poison leaves you in a state of vulnerability. Remain vigilant; watch constantly; and be fully aware, as a warrior in the heat of the battle.

WARFARE

In times of warfare, the Lord has revealed to me that others had been assigned to the same battle, and I was not fighting independently. They were fighting when I was unaware or couldn't fight alone. On one occasion, the Lord assured me He had commissioned four other intercessors to fight with me. Because of that, the fight was intense but short. Within minutes, I felt release and victory because of the concentrated effort, and visions regarding the Lord's plans were seen clearly. The enemy's attempt to put a screeching halt on God's plan will be quickly defeated when unity and intercession coincide. Second Corinthians 10:3-5 says,

> For although we live in the natural realm, we don't wage a military campaign employing human weapons, *using manipulation to achieve our aims.* Instead, our *spiritual* weapons are energized with divine power to effectively dismantle the defenses *behind which people hide.* We can demolish every deceptive fantasy that opposes God and break through every arrogant attitude that is raised up in defiance of the true

knowledge of God. We capture, like prisoners of war, every thought and insist that it bow in obedience to the Anointed One (TPT).

Recently Rob and I were pulling weeds around our home and got into poison ivy. What began as a tad bit uncomfortable morphed into a monster of a rash, spreading across our arms, legs, and torsos, leaving us scratching for weeks. We learned more about poison ivy during that fiasco than the simple, "stay away from the three leaves" rule we were taught as children. Not only is the plant itself a menace, but its oils can be found on the trees and plants surrounding the ivy. Pets can carry it into the home; it can be carried in the air; it sticks to your clothing; and its oil can linger on tools for years if not cleaned properly.

After several days of covering ourselves in Calamine lotion, anger rose, and I decided right then and there I would find that stupid ivy plant and destroy it, eliminating any chance of reliving this debacle. Gloved up and on a mission, I marched around the yard searching for the culprit that put us in this predicament. Making multiple trips around the property with no luck, I threw my hands in the air admitting defeat. Returning to the house with a deflated ego, I decided to stop at the mailbox before going inside to sulk in my annoyance and agonizing itch. And there it was, right below the mailbox. I spotted the dreaded three-leaf plant, not where we had been pulling weeds, but snuggled up at the one spot we visited daily. It was weaving its way up the tree as if it were staring me down and laughing at the victory it had just won. I was fit to be tied. I pulled it up by the roots and doused the ground with a gallon of weed killer. I was determined that silly plant would pay for what it did to us!

Moving back the branches to ensure I had rid ourselves of the weed, I saw a nest with two doves tucked away. Like the ivy, they were hidden in a place we frequently passed. In a small way, that poison ivy reminded me of times of warfare, where we are required to face ugly conditions, confront our enemies, and endure until we see victory. During warfare, the Father's promises can be seen when you look deep, knowing His sweet Spirit is always with you, even deep in the middle of the poison. My mom would say, "The enemy will wrap up poison as an inviting present, once unwrapped, it will wreak havoc on your life. But if you look closely, the Father will have your promise waiting for you in the middle of your battle. First, you must open your spiritual eyes to see. It's right there."

When He calls us into warfare and intercession, He fights alongside never leaving us alone. His Spirit, although in the middle of the war zone, rests comfortably in the knowledge of His victory, just as the doves rested under the ivy. First Peter 3:22 encourages us, "Jesus has the last word on everything and everyone, from angels to armies. He's standing right alongside God, and what he says goes" (MSG).

I believe the words of President Bush regarding the war on terrorism depict the attitude we must operate in regarding warfare: "The battle is joined on many fronts. We will not waver; we will not tire; we will not falter, and we will not fail." Trust Him within your war, regardless of what you see in the natural. He will hit His gavel, bring all chaos to a screeching halt, and stand with you victorious.

10
Trust During Change

*For everyone who knows your wonderful name keeps
putting their trust in you.
They can count on you for help no matter what.
O Lord, you will never, no never,
neglect those who come to you*
(Psalm 9:10 TPT).

Change was a new concept for me, considering I had lived in the same home most of my life. Passing on several opportunities for promotions, Dad had kept change far from our lives. The biggest adjustment we faced was advancing from elementary to high school. All that to say, when I married Rob, I was abruptly thrust into a world of change. We have now lived in 11 different homes together, and I have learned to thrive on the change and challenges. It helped that I enjoyed meeting new people, settling in new homes, and beginning new ministries. But it didn't always come easily. Our move to New Mexico, for instance, was particularly difficult. Leaving my parents, grandparents, and siblings behind as we moved across the country was hard. Two of our children embraced the change, and two were not as convinced. But an even more difficult change than that cross-country move was unloading our children at college. Four times we have decorated a new dorm room and driven away. Change can be hard.

But I have learned that how you approach change is vital to the success of the transition. Finding your equilibrium, even though you are shaking, will keep you levelheaded. It does not matter how many hurdles stand in the way, trusting the Father during these seasons is imperative and can keep you from emotional and mental strain.

In 2005, Rob and I were raising our little crew in Oklahoma City. This appointment was our first full-time assignment as state youth and discipleship directors for the Church of God. We were no longer serving at a local church, but our new focus was directed toward evangelism, missions, and youth. During our two years there, we met amazing people, worked long hours, and fought brutal spiritual warfare. In many ways, it was our most challenging assignment, yet I look back on those two short years as the most influential and developing years of my life. Rob was gone more than either of us wanted, but God was always by our sides. There were challenges and obstacles around every corner it seemed, but the Lord was ever-present, aligning our hearts to His.

During that time, I was quite busy with toddlers, homeschooling, and life in general. The house had carpet in the kitchen, which was a nightmare with young ones. The light from the bay window showed every speck of grimy dirt that little fingers left behind, making cleaning a hassle. Staying "caught up" felt impossible. I was often overwhelmed, but we experienced miracle after miracle during that season. One day, in all honesty, I was at my wit's end. It seemed as if everything that could go wrong, did go wrong, and tensions were high. One of the many issues I was dealing with was our garbage disposal. It had been out of commission for four days. I had tried everything to fix it, but nothing worked. The only option left was calling a repairman, which meant spending money we did not have at the time.

I gathered the children around the sink and explained to them that God cared about every detail of our lives, and He was perfectly able to heal our garbage disposal. I will never forget anointing their little hands with oil as we gathered around the disposal and prayed, "God, we ask by morning this machine work properly." The next morning the children could not wait to see if God had answered our prayers. I remember saying, "Lord, please use this small, somewhat insignificant machine to teach my children that You care about everything in our lives. I know You can heal this garbage disposal." If I am being completely truthful, I held my breath as I flipped the switch the next morning. God showed Himself faithful that day as the garbage disposal revved to life, and the children and I did victory laps around the kitchen. From the small to the great, God was there to steady the ship and bring peace and encouragement to our home during this season of change.

Another time God intervened was when Rob was on a fourteen-day missions trip to Africa. The schedule had no mercy, and life never slowed down. In the middle of the craziness, our dryer stopped working. For some reason, this pushed me over the edge. I felt frustrated, stressed, exhausted, and in no mood for this fiasco. While I was washing dishes, I complained out loud to the Lord, "I am sick of being so far from my family; I am tired of doing all this alone; I can't do this anymore." As my complaining tirade continued, I began hearing the sweet little voices of my children praying in the laundry room, which was adjacent to the kitchen. I stopped what I was doing and looked around the corner to see their hands on the dryer and their heads bowed in prayer, asking the Lord to heal our dryer so I would not be worried anymore. My heart melted, and I began praying and agreeing with them. Of course, the Lord showed off for my little ones one more time, and the dryer immediately began working!

Yes, I believe God heals inanimate objects for His glory and the loving care of His people. While Rob was away, God was watching out for us, taking care of what some would call "insignificant items," but it was important for our little family. In the grand scheme of things, these were small annoyances, but He understood where I was in life and the massive changes I was facing. His everyday interactions were divinely orchestrated for our family, and they helped me avoid discouragement, and keep my focus on what was truly important. He was our provider, our healer, and our trusted companion through every changing season.

LET'S GO

In Matthew 4:18-22, Jesus called His disciples to leave their entire lives behind and follow Him.

> As Jesus was walking beside the Sea of Galilee, he saw two brothers, Simon called Peter and his brother Andrew. They were casting a net into the lake, for they were fishermen. "Come, follow me," Jesus said, "and I will send you out to fish for people." At once they left their nets and followed him. Going on from there, he saw two other brothers, James son of Zebedee and his brother John. They were in a boat with their father Zebedee, preparing their nets. Jesus called them, and immediately they left the boat and their father and followed him (NIV).

The disciples were about to go on the ride of their lives, and no questions were asked. They had a, "Let's go!" mentality. Verse 20 says, "at once they left their nets," and verse

22 says, "Immediately they left the boat and their father and followed him." Jesus' compelling command gave the disciples the courage to leave their lives behind to be with a man, they did not know. All that had happened in their lives before was simply preparation for this next season. Change may have brought fear, but obedience was their first instinct.

Will we obey without question, with an *at-once* attitude? Or do we want to play it safe and stay on the path of least resistance? Can we allow our will to converge with the Father's? Can we hand Him the reins and submit to His changes in our lives? Life is full of forks in our path, and sometimes we must make difficult decisions.

THE WILLOW

When I think of adapting, my mind goes to the research I did on the weeping willow tree. As a young girl, I would lie under a willow and daydream for hours. They remind me of carefree, happy-go-lucky days as a child. Researching the tree, I learned how adaptive they are. They have strong roots; they have a thick, scaly bark that offers protection from the elements; mature trees can survive drought; and they can easily bend without breaking. One of the most interesting facts is the healing nature of the willow's bark. It can be used for several issues: swelling associated with an injury, arthritis, fever, headaches, muscular pain, cramps, flu-like symptoms, cuts, burns, and as a blood thinner.

Hippocrates, a physician who lived in ancient Greece in the fifth century B.C., discovered some of these medicinal qualities. He found that willow bark, when chewed, could lower fever and reduce pain. Native Americans also discovered some of the healing properties of willow bark and used it to treat fever, arthritis, headaches, and toothaches.

Edward Stone, a British minister, did experiments in 1763 on willow bark and leaves and identified and isolated salicylic acid. The acid caused too much stomach upset to be widely used until 1897, when a chemist named Felix Hoffman created a synthetic version that was gentle on the stomach. Hoffman called his invention "aspirin" and produced it for his company—Bayer.

Once while facing spiritual changes, I was challenged as I considered this tree and its characteristics. Was I adaptive or resistant to change? Would I describe my roots as strong, aggressive, and deep, able to withstand seasons of drought without bending? Do others want to be around me because I offer relief? Does the healing of my Father rub off on them? Not wanting to circumvent these questions, but knowing they would lead to more change, I was hesitant to address my weaknesses. The Father continued to nudge me toward my issues, giving me the strength to take a more offensive posture concerning them. Truth is, at the time, I was not adapting well to the changes I was facing. I felt anything but strong; however, staying in that position was not an option. Arriving at your full potential with the Father is always His goal, and He will lovingly push you until mediocre no longer satisfies.

At that time, change was a necessity for growth in my spiritual life. I had become comfortable, somewhat stagnant, and the worst part, I was completely unaware. Revealing my closemindedness concerning the way the Father spoke to me, He lovingly guided me into a time of change to expand my dependence on Him. I leaned heavily on dreams and visions, and the Lord longed to teach me to hear His voice in other ways. I had become off-balanced and looked to my dreams before prayer and the Word. My God-given dreams came to a screeching halt, and they were absent for almost two years.

> ❝ *Arriving at your full potential with the Father is always His goal, and He will lovingly push you until mediocre no longer satisfies.* ❞

I grieved over the dreams stopping, but the Father reassured me that this season of change and reset did not mean He was not moving. He was moving, but in a different way than the one to which I was accustomed. Change and stretching were what I needed. I had become dependent upon the way I heard from Him when, at my disposal, was an array of gifts He wanted to give. He was not stopping my dreams per se, but He was strengthening spiritual gifts that had become dormant. I had to be willing to recognize life's natural ebb and flow and be willing to adapt and bend like the willow tree to grow spiritually with the Father and to be able to bring His healing to others. In Song of Solomon 2:13, we can hear the excitement as the lover says,

> "Can you not discern this new day of destiny breaking forth around you? The early signs of my purposes and plans are bursting forth. The budding vines of new life are now blooming everywhere. The fragrance of their flower's whispers, 'There is change in the air.' Arise, my love, my beautiful companion, and run with me to the higher place. For now, is the time to arise and come away with me" (TPT).

Change is coming, yes, but never forget the purpose is to run with Him to a higher place.

HOT COFFEE, COLD MILK

I staggered toward the coffee pot early one morning, when I heard little feet stampeding down the stairs. My grandson excitedly asked the routine question, "Hot coffee, cold milk time?" His sweet voice carried throughout the house, full of carefree energy and ready to conquer a new day. Being the oldest, Elisha explained to his younger sister the necessity of "Cici" getting her morning coffee before any fun could begin. I prepared their milk topped with Ready Whip, while they both jumped around the kitchen dramatically describing their dreams. I couldn't help but laugh at their wild imaginations. Mornings, when my grandchildren come to visit, can be a fantastic adventure!

With our drinks in hand, we moved to the front porch and snuggled close in a cozy blanket. We discussed important life issues—the changing colors of the leaves, what the birds might be saying to us as they sang, and the sounds the rain made falling on the sidewalk. Then Elisha asked about his favorite Bible story.

"Tell me about Elisha in the Bible, Cici." I delved right into the dramatic scene of Naaman the warrior knocking on the prophet Elisha's door. He fully expected a miracle, but the response he received was somewhat disappointing. We reenacted the entire story with silly motions, "And on the seventh dip, he came out of the water clean!" Our "Hot coffee, cold milk time" was fun, but as we moved forward with the rest of our day, I continued to ponder Naaman's story. I found myself frustrated at his lack of immediate obedience. I thought, *If I had leprosy, I would be willing to do anything!* The Lord gently began working on my heart revealing there were times when I said I trusted Him, but my actions proved otherwise. Gut punch.

Learning to Trust the Father's Heart

Although Naaman was a victorious commander of the Syrian army, a man revered and honored, he experienced a drastic change. At some point in his life, he went from healthy to leprous. In 2 Kings 5:11, Naaman said, "I thought that he would surely come out to me and stand and call on the name of the Lord his God, wave his hand over the spot and cure me of my leprosy" (NIV). This leads you to believe he was in the beginning stages of the disease. Even so, he knew the prognosis was grim, and he would lose everything he had worked and fought for. Surely, he was desperate to be healed.

He was now required to submit to the authority and instructions of an unfamiliar prophet. Naaman was leaving his title at Elisha's door and abdicating his control to a God he did not know. No wonder he struggled. It was not a natural response, nor was it his first. In verses 13-14, Naaman's servants went to him and said,

> "My father, if the prophet had told you to do some great thing, would you not have done it? How much more, then, when he tells you, 'Wash and be cleansed'!" So he went down and dipped himself in the Jordan seven times, as the man of God had told him, and his flesh was restored and became clean like that of a young boy (NIV).

His servants had to convince him to let go of anger and obey the prophet. Naaman was required to push through his expectations and accept the uncomfortable and excruciatingly awkward requirement.

Change must take place to allow room for the new. Sometimes, like Naaman, we believe we are strong and deserve the best, and we have to be humbled to be restored. Other times we are like Gideon and believe that we are weak and incapable and must be convinced that the Lord can bless us and use us. Judges 6:14-15 says. "The Lord turned to him and said, 'Go in the strength you have and save Israel out of Midian's hand. Am I not sending you?' 'Pardon me, my lord,' Gideon replied, 'but how can I save Israel? My clan is the weakest in Manasseh, and I am the least in my family'" (NIV).

> **" Change must take place to allow room for the new. "**

Gideon believed he was the weakest and could never accomplish anything of worth. His trust in God was fragile, and God was in the process of transforming Gideon from a follower to a leader. This was a change that he couldn't wrap his mind around. Leading when you feel unworthy and un-prepared is overwhelming. All eyes were looking to Gideon for answers, all while he was waiting for the answers him-self. God equipped Gideon for the major life-changes, and He will do the same for you. Proverbs 19:21 says, "Many plans occupy the mind of a man, but the Lord's purposes will prevail" (ISV).

REST IN HIS ARMS

On a recent flight to New York, I found myself watching a television series, *The Men Who Built America: Frontiers-man*. I was intrigued by their willingness to begin again, changing their lives completely, all in hopes of money and land. Many would risk their lives for the new frontier and wide-open spaces that were ready to be conquered. One man the series highlighted was Daniel Boone. They told the story of his daughter, Jemima, who had been captured by a raiding party. Her father had trained her to survive in any situation. Trusting her instincts, she sneakily left pieces of her dress as a trail for him to find her. She kept a level head, leaned on her training, and waited for her father to arrive. He did arrive, found his daughter, and saved her life from her enemy.

It is no understatement to say change is intense, difficult to maneuver, and often a hard pill to swallow. Even when we are diligently searching for the positives, the negatives can be glaring. Jesus brings rest in the middle of change. How? His perfect peace casts out all fear. Rest in His arms. We begin life being held in the secure arms of our parents. This is where the Lord wants us, in His secure, strong, and loving arms—trusting completely.

But we don't always rest there. Have you ever tried to hold down a fighting baby? That's the visual I get of the Father trying to bring comfort when we insist on fighting. Or it's like a fish out of water, flopping around out of its element. We gasp for air and try to fix what is out of our control. He says rest, and we fight back, believing our flopping and panting will somehow help our circumstances. Philippians 4:6 says, "Do not be anxious about anything, but in every situation, by prayer and petition, with thanksgiving, present your requests to God. And the peace of God, which transcends all understanding, will guard your hearts and your minds in Christ Jesus" (NIV).

His rest goes beyond our best attempt at understanding. He sees and knows not only the situation but every detail about each person involved. He sees the big picture. This means not only does He know where we are now, but He also knows where we are going and the changes involved. This knowledge protects our hearts and minds if we will allow ourselves to rest in Him.

Change is where I found Him, not only in the dream or vision but also in the stillness. While in quiet places, I first thought I had been deserted. As I looked closer, though, I truly discovered Him, His sweetness, His embrace, and His reassuring love. Just as Daniel Boone's daughter trusted her father with her whole heart, knowing he would rescue her, so must we trust what resides within our hearts. Regardless of the changes we face, He will show up on our behalf.

11
Trust With Your Heart

You will keep him in perfect peace,
whose mind is stayed on You,
because he trusts in You
(Isaiah 26:3).

"I trust You, Lord. I trust You with all my heart."

He responded, "Your children are your heart. Do you trust Me with them?"

The most magical moments of my life were holding our babies for the first time. Each time I was physically exhausted, and yet I was wrapped in the ambiance of wonder as we counted fingers and toes. We laughed and cried at the same time. As I looked at each of them, the strenuous voyage of pregnancy and labor seemed like a sidenote, if anything. They were worth all the struggle and pain. I could not avert my eyes from them for even a second. Few things in life compare to those four precious babies, and I never believed I could experience anything remotely close to it until I witnessed my grandchildren take their first breaths. Rob and I beamed with pride as we saw the future of our family in their sweet faces.

When we received the news about becoming grandparents, immediately my thoughts went to what my daughter would endure. When she announced the baby would be born at home, not in the hospital, I struggled. Tense about the decision, my mind was swirling, "So many things could go wrong. How do we know how she will handle the pain? What if there are complications? Will a midwife know how to handle an emergency?" Having been with my sister, Farah, at her home birth, I had some knowledge and leaned heavily on that for peace. I tried my best to stay positive and to reassure myself and Rob that it would all be okay. I tried to constrain my fear and trust God to take care of her and the baby.

When the big day arrived, I had preconceptions about how it would play out. One was that she would have a quick labor like both my mother and I had. However, when we reached hour ten and still had little progress, I knew her birthing process would not follow the same pattern. The sounds of her pain loomed over me and left me feeling helpless. My sister is a doula and assists moms during labor. She was with us before the contractions even began and helped every step of the way. When we were depleted of all our energy, she was like the energizer bunny, still going. Out of my daughter's earshot, I expressed to her that I was feeling wildly desperate to see her progress, and we needed to do something. She explained the Natural Alignment Plateau to me. It is a normal stall in dilation. Farah assured me that transition was close at hand, and I would soon hold my grandson. What appeared to me like nothing was happening, in actuality, was preparation for rapid dilation. To encourage this concerned momma, she said, "Trust that her body knows what to do. Just be patient and believe."

Forcing a smile to disguise my concern, I pushed on. All I could do was love my daughter and be there close by. I was unable to take her pain, accelerate the time, or change the circumstances. Trust and believe, that was all I had. How could that possibly be enough? Suddenly, I understood what my husband meant when he said he felt desperate when I was giving birth. Thankfully, Farah understood the process, and as expected, our grandson arrived safe and sound. Even so, I will never forget my daughter's cries for help.

I have heard the same groans of pain from mothers crying out for God to again deliver their child, this time from the abysmal pit of sin. They are unable to take away the pain, accelerate time, or change circumstances for their child. But like my sister, the Holy Spirit reminds them to, "only trust and believe." Both mothers and fathers wrestle with the ability to release their child into God's hands. It's a task that is much easier said than done.

SUPERHERO DAD

I enjoy getting on YouTube and watching Superman dads—hero compilations. Dads come on the scene and save their children, inches from disaster. Most dads have similar stories, and they are awesome to watch. Around 18 months of age, I decided to jump, face first, out of my dad's light blue '62 Chevy pickup truck. Mom and I were running errands with Dad on a hot summer day. My mom and I were going to wait in the truck with the windows down, while he made a quick stop at the post office. After being told, "Stay with Mom this time, Baby," I began to cry, insisting on going in with him. As he shut the door, I took a nosedive out the window. Dad's spontaneous reflexes kicked in, catching me by my foot as my hair swept the ground.

We have a similar story with our daughter, Lexi, while we lived in Albuquerque, New Mexico. She was two years old and never stopped moving. My husband's office was upstairs in the church we pastored, and getting to him with four children was not simple. I remember counting every concrete step out loud to teach our younger two children numbers, and to occupy the older two with a counting game. Now many years later, I cannot recall how many stairs there were, but I'm sure there were more than twenty. Those stairs were always a concern, and keeping the children away from them was a challenge. One Wednesday night after service, it was late, and we were trying our best to wrap up loose ends in the office. Lexi, with mischief in her eyes and her thumb in her mouth, took off running toward those stairs. Knowing it would not end well, Rob, in superhero fashion, literally leaped, soaring face-first down the stairs to catch her before she could be injured. Miraculously, he caught her by the ankle in mid-air, right before her little face met the concrete. I wish I had a videotape of my superhero husband, leaping down the staircase like Spider-Man!

> " *The simple truth is, we can't see the danger, pain, and heartache that is ahead of them, but He can. He is always faithful to act on their behalf.* "

How many times have we had "too close for comfort" situations with our children? Dad sweeps in and saves the day. Our heavenly Father does the same for His children. Resting in that assurance can be challenging for parents. With trepidation in our hearts, we must release our babies into the hands of the loving Father. The simple truth is, we can't see the danger, pain, and heartache that is ahead of them, but He can. He is always faithful to act on their behalf.

Satan has been given freedom to a degree, but like a dog on a leash, Father God pulls his restraints, reminding him who is truly the boss. The line is drawn in the sand as the Father announces, "That's enough; you go no farther." The enemy himself will admit his subordinate role and surrender in defeat when God's children call out to Him. When they cry out, the enemy whimpers, and there is no denying who the true King is. Satan must listen!

STEPS OF A GOOD FATHER

One of the most noteworthy fathers in the Bible is Job. His daily life and actions were influential as he led his children in the ways of God by example. Job 1 gives us a close-up look at how he ran his household and solidified his leadership as a father. We see his reverence for God and his heart for his children. Unable to control their actions, still he stepped in as the priest of his home, took action on their behalf, and represented God. Job 1:4-5 says,

> And his sons would go and feast in their houses, each on his appointed day, and would send and invite their three sisters to eat and drink with them. So it was, when the days of feasting had run their course, that Job would send and sanctify them, and he would rise early in the morning and offer burnt offerings according to the number of them all. For Job said, "It may be that my sons have sinned and cursed God in their hearts." Thus Job did regularly.

Job was a fantastic example of a father engaged in his children's lives. Suspecting that they might have sinned, he took immediate action. We can learn a great deal from the steps he took to ensure their righteousness before God.

First, Job sent for his children, keeping the lines of communication open. By doing so, they were fully aware of his commitment to the family. He didn't push them away. He stayed in contact with them, filling their primal need for love and acceptance from their father. Staying close to our children, even when we do not entirely agree on everything, speaks volumes to them. Consider 1 Peter 4:8, "Above all, love each other deeply, because love covers a multitude of sins" (NIV). "Above all," reminds us that nothing is more significant than giving them our love.

Second, he sanctified his children. The Bible does not say if this was done by praying or by instructing them to repent, but he was guiding them by example and fulfilling the role of the priest of his home with perseverance and dignity. In John 17:17, Jesus prayed, "Sanctify them by the truth; your word is truth" (NIV). Speaking the truth in love to our children moves their hearts toward the Father.

The third way he led his children to righteousness was by making them a priority. He showed that God and family come before all others. Not wasting a minute, as soon as his feet touched the ground, he went into action. Offering burnt offerings on behalf of each of his children, Job called out their names before God. Just in case there was even the thought of sin, he wanted them covered and was not willing to risk their righteousness with God.

Last, verse 5 says he followed these steps regularly, meaning he would not quit. Job was ready and willing to do whatever it took to make certain his family was walking in the ways of the Lord. His reassuring presence, faithful representation of God, and never-faltering love and devotion set a standard for his children to follow. Although no parent walks in perfection, and most would love to have a "re-do" at times—striving toward improvement should be a never-ending endeavor. Job's parenting style gives us an opportunity for self-examination. How do our communications, prayers, priorities, and consistencies line up with this wonderful Biblical example of parenting?

In complete contrast to Job, the Bible tells the story of a father in 1 Kings whose decadence and depravity are unimaginable. Heil has an unfathomable story. He built Jericho even after it had been cursed by Joshua. Completely disregarding the curse, he moved forward in his plans to rebuild, no matter the cost. For him, it was a massive price—the lives of his sons. First Kings 16:34 says, "In his days, Hiel the Bethelite built Jericho. He laid the foundation at the expense of his firstborn Abiram and set up the gates at the cost of the life of his youngest son Segub, according to the word of the Lord, which He spoke by Joshua the son of Nun" (MEV).

Hiel built a kingdom at the expense of his family. His eldest son died as they laid the foundation of the new Jericho. This proved without a doubt that the Word of the Lord was true, and yet he finished the project, allowing his youngest son to die as he set up the gates. The drastic differences between Job and Hiel are glaring. One father did what was best for his family; the other did what was best for himself. Hiel epitomized selfishness and greed, sacrificing his children, but Job epitomized selflessness as he cried out for the lives of his children, doing whatever he could to lead them to righteousness. His children could completely trust their father as he completely trusted his heavenly Father.

TRUSTING MOTHER

In the very next chapter, 1 Kings 17, we are introduced to a widow, who was fighting for her survival and that of her son during a drought. She was a desperate mother, full of fear, yet she obeyed the prophet Elijah when he asked her to feed him first. Stating the obvious in verse 12, she empathically told the prophet, "As the Lord your God lives, I do not have bread, but only a handful of meal in a barrel and a little oil in a jar. I am gathering two sticks, that I can go in and make it for me and my son, so we may eat it and die" (MEV).

Knowing they were in a life and death dilemma, he pushed her faith to its limits. He said to her in verses 13-14:

> "Do not fear; go and do as you have said, but make a little cake for me first, and bring it to me, and afterward, make some for your son and you, for thus says the Lord God of Israel: The barrel of meal will not run out, nor will the jar of oil empty, until the day that the Lord sends rain upon the earth" (MEV).

The prophet's response in these verses included a promise; however, I wonder if, under the same circumstances, I would be obedient to his command. If I were in the same situation, would I be uttering accusations under my breath while making his cake? "How selfish to put himself before my boy! What kind of holy man would take away our last hope?" His request was unrealistic, making survival for them impossible if she followed through. How could he ask for such a high price? The Father asks the same of us, "Will you surrender your plans for your children? Will you trust Me, even when the price seems too high?"

To say the least, Elijah and this mom's relationship began on shaky grounds. Pushing through her doubts and fears, she did obey, and their circumstances wholly turned around. Elijah's prayers, mixed with her obedience, created a miracle that would feed them while others were dying of hunger. The oil and meal did not run out, and God was true to His Word. However, this instance didn't cause her to believe Elijah was a man of God. Quoting from the *Modern English Version*, chapter 17 continues to tell the story of this little family, and the grief that soon followed. Verse 17 says, "Later on, [her] son . . . became terribly sick, so much so that he had no breath left in him." Her miracle boy, all she had left of her husband, was now dead, and she was angry. In verse 18, she said to Elijah, "What do I have to do with you, O you man of God? Have you come to remind me of my sin and to kill my son?" Elijah responded in verse 19 by saying, "Give me your son." He laid himself on the boy's body three times, and cried out to God, "O, Lord, my God, I pray that You let this child's soul come into him again" (v. 21). God heard his prayers, and according to verse 23, the prophet took the boy back to his mother and said, "See, your son lives!"

> " *Will you surrender your plans for your children? Will you trust Me, even when the price seems too high?* "

She *then* proclaimed, "Now, because of this, I know that you are a man of God and that the word of the Lord in your mouth is truth!" (v. 24). The provision of food did not open her eyes to see he was a man of God. It took new life. Yes, we provide for the physical needs of our children and thank God for the ability to do so. Do we trust Him enough to surrender their spiritually dead bodies to Him and believe for the miraculous? God is appealing to the hearts of parents, "Give me your children. Trust me with their lives."

You see, there's a difference in keeping someone breathing and putting new breath in them. Consider life support versus resurrection. Individuals on life support are still alive technically, but they aren't truly living. Are we just hooking up our children to machines, as it were, and allowing artificial air to bring the signs of life, when in reality, they are robotic, dull, and without vibrancy? Or, are we offering them the breath of the Father to resuscitate them? Are we encouraging them to find life like Jesus describes in the Book of John? "I have come that they may have life, and that they may have it more abundantly" (John 10:10). Anything less is unacceptable.

Nothing is more precious to a mother than her children. She will do anything for her child. They do not allow their little ones to get involved with just anyone. They must be assured they are safe. Elijah had proven to the widow that he was trustworthy, so when there was no chance for survival, she trusted him, and it led to resurrection power that brought her dead son back to life. In our world today, it looks bleak, and parents are saying there is no chance for resurrection; we see no hope for change. But I hear confidence rising as God says, "Give me the child." When we surrender our wisdom to the Father and trust Him to breathe new life into our children, victory becomes possible. He has proven to us that He is trustworthy, hasn't He? So we must let go, release our babies into His hands, and believe.

PRISONERS LISTEN

Not only must we release our lost children into His hands, but we must also trust His timing. That, I believe, can be most difficult. "I trust You and know You have a plan, but when?" A prison sentence is easier to handle when there's a release date given. Being able to count down the days to freedom makes the sentence somewhat more tolerable. The problem is—it is out of the prisoner's control, and the wait can be painstakingly slow. Proverbs 13:12 says, "Hope deferred makes the heart sick" (ESV).

With a lost loved one, we are crying out for someone who does not realize he or she is in prison. Unknowingly, this loved one lives in a cage of sin with the keys to freedom in his or her own hands. What they are thinking? Do they think the motivations of their hearts are not known, leaving those on the outside of the cage with a dull ache inside? We, as parents, could endure their sentence a little more easily if the release date were given. The problem is—the length of the imprisonment is out of our control, and the wait can be unbearable. When we do not know the date, we must trust the timing to God, because He does know the date of their release. He also knows how and when it will happen, and the plan He has for them afterward.

He assures us in 2 Peter 3:9: "The Lord is not slow concerning His promise, as some count slowness. But He is patient with us, because He does not want any to perish, but all to come to repentance" (MEV). We do not possess the ability within ourselves to bring back our prodigals, but trusting His plan to pick them up out of the miry clay is our only and best option. We must be willing to wait and give Him a chance to work. But where does that leave us while we wait? What's our command? Needing a compass to guide, I asked the Father, and He led me to Acts 16:25: "About midnight Paul and Silas were praying and singing hymns to God, and the other prisoners were listening to them" (NIV).

With heartfelt hope, He focused my attention on the last portion of this scripture. Prisoners listen! Prisoners of sin and bondage, chained, and confined to the jail of shame . . . listen. The Bible does not disclose all the details, but knowing it was midnight, certainly, prisoners were awakened by the sounds of Paul and Silas. They may have been perturbed at first; however, the vacancy in their hearts must have responded to the peace that filled that jail cell. A presence uncommon to their dreary surroundings grabbed their attention.

> **" *We do not possess the ability within ourselves to bring back our prodigals, but trusting His plan to pick them up out of the miry clay is our only and best option.* "**

Just as those prisoners in Philippi, our loved ones may be asleep and reluctant to be awakened; however, they will respond to the presence of God, because it is a vast contrast to where they currently are. They may not listen to our debating or opinions, but they will listen to the peace and presence that comes from prayers and singing.

Although we strive to reach them with our weighty words full of wisdom and truth, our efforts pale in comparison to the chain-breaking power of His presence. Words are heard and at times even acknowledged, but it takes God's glory to chisel away at the hardened heart. Acts 16:26 says, "Suddenly there was a great earthquake, so that the foundations of the prison were shaken. And immediately all the doors were opened and everyone's shackles were loosened" (MEV).

Prayer and worship move the heart of God, but they can also move the heart of the lost, resulting in chain-breaking deliverances. Why else would the enemy discourage you from prayer and worship? Why does he taunt believers with thoughts of, "They are too far gone? Your prodigal cannot be reached. Their pit is too dark. Their sin is too heavy." When the enemy spews these lies to you, remind him what God has to say about Leviathan! Leviathan is a creature with no fear, yet it bows and is under subjection to the Father. Job 41:33 states, "Nothing on earth is its equal, no other creature so fearless" (NLT). God speaks, and Leviathan must listen. No spirit is too strong for our God. No sin can survive in His presence. Psalm 74:14 says, "You crushed the heads of Leviathan; you gave him as food for the creatures of the wilderness" (ESV). As He did with Leviathan, our Father will destroy the enemy that wars against our families, and every evil that has fought against our homes will bow before our God.

Debilitating bondage does not exist in His presence; only supreme love and peace. He can and will easily crush the head of the enemies fighting our prisoners. No spirit is too strong for our God. No one is out of reach or too far gone. If Leviathan must listen, so must the spirits of this world that hold our children and loved ones in bondage. Prayer and worship loosen the chains. We worship and appeal to our Father on behalf of our lost loved ones. We kneel in prayer and rise with unwavering faith that eradicates Satan's plan. Nothing will stop the homeward march of the prodigal. Nothing!

Prisoners listen to the Father, despite what we see, feel, or hear. God has the last word. Just as the woman handed her dead son to Elijah, we hand our lifeless sons and daughters to the Lord and trust Him to bring them back to life. Not just for our babies, but God also has plans for the nation as He did for Israel. Looking at 1 Kings 18, we see God beginning to bring resurrection to lifeless bodies. His plan was much larger than only the widow's son. He wanted the nation.

The heinous sins of Ahab and Jezebel had left the nation of Israel spiritually dead. The rain had not fallen in three years, and the earth was as dry and parched as the hearts of the people. The time had come for God to show who the true king was. Elijah was at war with the false god Baal on Mount Carmel, as all the children of Israel watched. Some

450 prophets of Baal, with all their fanfare, had begged Baal for six hours to respond with fire, but this fabricated god was no match for the true King. With a short, earnest prayer, Elijah eradicated every doubt in the people's minds. God showed up with fire and won back the heart of His nation. First Kings 18:39 says, "Now when all the people saw it, they fell on their faces; and they said, 'The LORD, He is God! The LORD, He is God!'"

The enemy has had his say for long enough, and Father God is stepping on the scene, grabbing His children from their downward spiral. Do not fear, your children will move from hiding to shining! Consider the progress of teaching them to swim. As they cautiously wade in the shallow waters, they doubt. Wide eyes, full of uncertainty, stare right at you, silently communicating their apprehensions and objections. You reassure them, "You can do this. Trust me. You're not alone." Despite the fear, they continue to want to test the water. We continue to push them out of their comfort zones, little by little building trust.

What begins with fear and hiding, ends with competent swimmers. Soon they want everyone to watch their cannonballs into the deep end. The Father is taking the lost through this process of trust as well. Remember 1 John 4:18: "There is no fear in love; but perfect love casts out fear, because fear involves torment." Don't be afraid; trust God with your children's hearts. He has a plan. Find hope in Hebrews 10:35-39:

> It's *still* a sure thing! But you need to stick it out, staying with God's plan so you'll be there for the promised completion.
>
> It won't be long now, he's on the way; he'll show up most any minute.

Learning to Trust the Father's Heart

But anyone who is right with me thrives
on loyal trust; if he cuts and runs, I
won't be very happy.

But we're not quitters who lose out. Oh, no!
We'll stay with it and survive, trusting all the
way (MSG).

We will not quit or be afraid! We will trust and stick this out because our Father is in control. Yes, we are unable to take their pain, accelerate the time, or change the circumstances, but, what is more important, we *can* trust and believe!

12
Trust Up the Mountain

Look! I'm setting a stone in Zion, a cornerstone in the place of honor. Whoever trusts in this stone as a foundation will never have cause to regret it. To you who trust him, he's a Stone to be proud of, but to those who refuse to trust him, the stone the workmen threw out is now the chief foundation stone. For the untrusting it's . . . a stone to trip over, a boulder blocking the way. They trip and fall because they refuse to obey, just as predicted
(1 Peter 2:6-8 MSG).

My dad and my son Tobie are both huge history buffs and love a good documentary, especially if it's about war. They could watch for hours, learning how territories were conquered and strategic war plans were created. They educate themselves on mistakes that were made, gaining understanding behind the mindset and tactics of the warring generals. It keeps them on the edge of their seats. Despite my lack of interest, I have learned a great deal about the difficulties of war and the sacrifices that must take place to walk away victorious.

In Joshua 17, the Promised Land was being divided, and portions were given to each tribe. Ephraim and Manasseh were not pleased with the property allotment they received. Because the Lord had blessed them, they were numerous people. Therefore, they did not feel they had been given enough land, and they asked for another allotment. Because of their numbers, Joshua conceded and gave them their allotment plus the forested hill country, but it came with some conditions. Joshua said, "The mountain country shall be yours. Although it is wooded, you shall cut it down, and its farthest extent shall be yours; for you shall drive out the Canaanites, though they have iron chariots and are strong" (v. 18). Along with the land came the responsibility of ridding it of the enemy, as well as clearing the land of trees, stumps, rocks, and debris. To say that they were not thrilled with their newly acquired lot in life is an understatement! Even though they had inherited a considerable share of land, they felt shortchanged and sorry for themselves.

" *We can always trust Him for good gifts, but rarely do they come easily.* **"**

They had the largest portion of land at their disposal, but because of the strength of their enemies, they perceived that they were incapable of defeating them and conquering the territory. The land was given as requested; however, the blessing would require not only work but also war. I would imagine they were excited when they learned they would get a large allotment, but when they saw the land, they may have felt that it was outside their capability. They may have become overwhelmed with fear and disappointment, or perhaps they questioned, "Wait . . . what is this? Haven't we worked enough? Shouldn't this territory be easy to obtain?"

When the Father responds to prayers, our excitement is over the top. When we are shown His answers, the obstacles and strongholds that come with the blessing are revealed. God often gives us the desire of our hearts, but when He entrusts us with His promises, we have no idea how difficult and cumbersome the required work will be. Excavating and clearing debris will ultimately make room for growth, expansion, and progress. It is easy to struggle with trusting Him through the excavation process. Clearing, weeding, and uprooting is labor-intensive and invasive, yet highly effective. It's unlikely that His gift is given without cost. I have discovered that we can always trust Him for good gifts, but rarely do they come easily.

Ephraim and Manasseh would be required to clear the land, and this hard work was not at all what these tribes had wanted. I'm sure they expected it to be easy, with no enemies, with good ground for farming, and most of all, free of labor. After all, they had waited many years, and their underlying assumption must have been that they deserved the best. Chances are, they weren't moldable toward this new idea and the work they would now incur. Feeling out of kilter, the people had to change their mindset and remember the many promises God had given them already. Deuteronomy 11:23 says, "Then the LORD will drive out all these nations from before you, and you will dispossess nations greater and mightier than you" (NASB 1995). "Know therefore today that it is the LORD your God who is crossing over before you as a consuming fire. He will destroy them and He will subdue them before you, so that you may drive them out and destroy them quickly, just as the LORD has spoken to you" (Deuteronomy 9:3 NASB 1995). The onslaught of the enemy may be unprecedented, and the how and why may not be known, even so, you can and will conquer!

RESETS

The Father is giving us the mountains and the territories we have asked Him for, but not without a cost. Trudging up the mountain and snatching it away from the enemy is bittersweet. Not only that, but the people you are required to work with on the journey can be disappointing. Many years earlier, Moses had experienced disappointment while he was on Mount Sinai receiving the Ten Commandments. His mountaintop experience was interrupted when God's anger rose against the people. Exodus 32:7 says, "The Lord said to Moses: Hurry back down! Those people you led out of Egypt are acting like fools" (CEV). In an instant, a beautiful moment between God and man took the back seat to rectify the sin of the people.

What Moses was thinking coming down that mountain, I don't know, but I assume by his actions, he was pretty infuriated. Exodus 32:19 says, "As Moses got closer to the camp, he saw the idol, and he also saw the people dancing around. This made him so angry that he threw down the stones and broke them to pieces at the foot of the mountain" (CEV). Enraged by the actions of the people, Moses lost control and did the unthinkable. He mishandled the words God had written.

Exodus 34:1 says, "One day the Lord said to Moses, 'Cut two flat stones like the first ones I made, and I will write on them the same commandments that were on the two you broke'" (CEV). Here's what I love about this passage—although Moses was unable to keep a level head, the Father gave him a do-over, not letting his anger ban him from service. Never be convinced you have caused irreversible damage to the Father's words over your life. He is the best at resetting destinies as you rise stronger and all that was lost is restored with a greater manifestation of

His glory. Listen to Exodus 34:29, "Moses came down from Mount Sinai, carrying the Ten Commandments. His face was shining brightly because the Lord had been speaking to him. But Moses did not know at first that his face was shining" (CEV).

"*Never be convinced you have caused irreversible damage to the Father's words over your life.* **"**

What the people saw the first time around was a face of anger and rage. God did not allow Moses' errors to disqualify him. Instead, He said, "Let's try this one more time: Get two more stones, and meet me again." This time a different man came down the mountain. After the second attempt, the people no longer saw fury, rather a face shining in God's glory. Reality is, we all succumb to pitfalls on our journey, often feeling as if we have destroyed the words God has spoken over our lives. Refuse to descend into the dark valley of regret, foregoing the mountain of glory He says you are worthy to climb. Accept forgiveness, dust yourself off, and go back up the mountain to meet with Him. Grappling with unworthiness and insecurities get you nowhere. Give yourself credit, and believe that through the Father's love and forgiveness, you can attain even greater than what was lost. His promises will be fulfilled in your life. Don't be afraid to follow Him again up the mountain, receiving your reset and coming back more ferociously on fire than the previous encounter you thought could not be topped. Take your eyes off your mistake, and trust the Father to again oversee your ascent. Moses carried the commandments.

What mandates do you carry? Just as the children of Israel recognized the glory on Moses' face, you too will be known for the glory you carry.

> " *Give yourself credit, and believe that through the Father's love and forgiveness, you can attain even greater than what was lost.* "

Psalm 125:1-2 says, "Those who trust in God are like Zion Mountain: Nothing can move it, a rock-solid mountain you can always depend on. Mountains encircle Jerusalem, and God encircles his people—always has and always will" (MSG).

FOLLOWING THE FATHER

My sweet grandfather went to be with the Lord this past year, leaving my dad, the eldest child, as the patriarch of our family. It overjoyed my dad to organize a hike in honor of his father to the old homestead where my great-great-grandparents had raised twelve children, now in the Smoky Mountain National Park. He pulled together as many family members as he could to visit this place of our heritage. The history of our family has great significance to my dad. He has spent untold hours researching his lineage, meeting with those ancestors still living, and collecting precious artifacts.

Following Dad as he led our family on this afternoon hike, I quickly realized the hike itself was not that difficult; however, maneuvering around the obstacles would prove to be the real challenge. For instance, while walking through the wooded areas, we were covered in clusters of prickly burrs, which we didn't notice until we felt hundreds of little, uncomfortable stings on our legs. We found ourselves avoiding rocks that would cause us to stumble and lose our balance, watching for potholes that could trip us or cause us to twist our ankles, and always staying mindfully aware of the drop-off. Not to mention, because this was a horse trail, we were weaving in and out of horse manure and puddles. The smart hikers were equipped with walking sticks and boots, but those of us who were not so prepared had to keep our eyes wide open or regret would quickly set in. All of this to say, if you are not watchful on your journey, you will find yourself in a real mess.

Along the way, we had to wait on one another and assist those behind us by clearing a path and lending a helping hand. Oftentimes, thorny branches would impede our chosen pathway. When walking on a path like this, there is a real temptation to simply push the branch out of one's way. The irony, of course, is that if you hold the branch for yourself and not for those following you, the thorny branch is propelled like a catapult into the face of whoever is following behind. It would be better for the individual to be walking alone than to be following a careless leader! But a certain symbiotic synergy is created as each hiker holds the branch for the next. When we climb like this, we learn to rely on each other.

Pushing through the thicket with no concern for those who follow gives the thorny branch momentum, and it not only creates deep wounds, but also slows them down on their journey. How? Not only are they struggling with the climb, but now they feel abandoned. Seeing you walking ahead and never bothering to look back, increases their difficulty as they are left to muscle through on an isolated climb. They are scrambling for answers and a helping hand, but they find themselves face down in the mud, trying to find their bearing.

As you climb on your Christian walk, be willing to be vulnerable and to serve and share with those climbing behind you. Listen, I get it. You don't want to expose every gory detail you face. That's not what I'm saying. You have been given an area of influence, and nothing can compare to the invaluable advice you can teach. If your approach is, "Well, they will just have to learn it the hard way," then it's time to reevaluate your heart. When we are okay with just taking care of ourselves, it's a sure sign there is a problem. Selfishness, even unknown to you, will make way for a lonesome journey, landing you on top of the mountain alone. Instead, walk with others on their trails: hurt with them, cry with them, bleed with them. If they will be teachable, then teach. If they will allow you to assist and train, then do so. Stop abandonment issues from having a place in your journey of faith. Stop caring about only yourself. Take what you learn from the journey and pass it on.

As our family reached our destination, I breathed in the crisp afternoon air, truly opened my eyes, and began to hear the voice of my Father. Gaining His perspective and allowing my mind to rise above the clutter of everyday life, I could see the beautiful symbolism on that mountain. The sun shone through the treetops onto the only things that remained of the 18 x 18 square-foot cabin structure—the cornerstone and the fireplace. "Look at what remains," I heard Him whisper to my spirit. The rock on which the structure was built, the cornerstone, and the place that produced fire. "My Son and my Spirit." Ephesians 2:20-22 says, "Having been built on the foundation of the apostles and prophets, Christ Jesus Himself being the chief cornerstone, in whom the whole building, being fitted together, grows into a holy temple in the Lord, in whom you also are being built together for a dwelling place of God in the Spirit."

> **"** *You have been given an area of influence, and nothing can compare to the invaluable advice you can teach.* **"**

My earthly father led our family on a journey to experience a family heirloom. Our heavenly Father leads us on a journey toward Him, where we experience Jesus, our chief cornerstone, and the Holy Spirit, our consuming fire. Not only did I see where my great-grandfather was born, but spiritually I saw the warmth and love of the Father. Once again, my dad, unknowingly, represented my heavenly Father, by teaching, training, and guiding his family.

The beauty of it consumes my emotions as his care and concern of every detail drives me to be a better representation of my Lord.

"DO YOU TRUST ME OR NOT?"

One year into the process of writing, I faced a fierce battle that was shaking my heart and mind. For three mornings in a row, I woke to those words. "Do you trust me or not?" I had been on a journey with my Father, which included painful moments as He gently revealed to me my lack of complete reliance on Him. Through His counsel, my growth exceeded that of the years I tried on my own. I was thankful for the teaching, pruning, and correction. Feeling I had made great headway, this question was posed. "Did I, or didn't I?" My choice. Will circumstances sway me? Is He God in the valley? Will He hold me in the storm?

That third morning my devotion was on Genesis 22 when God asked Abraham to trust Him with his son's life, and he began the mountain climb. Follow the Father and trust. The angel of the Lord stopped Abraham in verse 12: "Then He said, 'Do not lay your hands on the boy or do anything to him, because now I know that you fear God, seeing you have not withheld your only son from Me'" (MEV). I knew I had to lay the things I had withheld from Him on the altar and trust.

Trying to navigate your way through a restricted out-crop of rocks and debris, surrounded with the clutter of life, feeling claustrophobic and out of control because of the constraints on all sides, you still must climb. All you can see at times are the difficult circumstances around you, closing in and circling like a group of vultures scavenging for their next meal. Dig in your heels. See and believe the truth the Father speaks over your life. This is the climb up the mountain He has ordained for your life. You are well able to take control, clear the land, and slaughter the enemy.

Learning to navigate and trust God through the demands and restrictions of life's journey enables you to take the next mountain. We want the mountaintop experiences, but there will undoubtedly be a process and a climb. Don't get daunted out of striving for the land you desire, something He has promised. It belongs to you already, but you must activate courage and take the mountain. Others' dogma and your self-deprecation must be stopped so you can follow the Father's ironclad plan for your climb.

Conclusion

You will keep him in perfect peace,
whose mind is stayed on You, because he trusts in You.
Trust in the LORD forever, for in GOD the LORD
we have an everlasting rock
(Isaiah 26:3-4 MEV).

Our safe place is one where He will never leave or forsake us.

If you visited my dad today, more than likely you would find him working a crossword puzzle or in the basement tinkering with his tools—two of his favorite pastimes. As a carpenter in his own right, he has created many small projects throughout his life. One precious heirloom is a child-size Adirondack chair he built with my son Robbie when he was four years old. So naturally, after an unsuccessful search for the perfect front porch swing, and, knowing his abilities, I asked Dad, "Hey, what would you think about using your carpentry skills to make a swing for me?" Amused he replied, "Well, let me see what I can do." I knew that meant yes. For the sake of clarification—if we ever have a reasonable request that is anywhere near his scope of capability, he finds a way to make it happen.

From childhood on, swinging has always been the place I relaxed and daydreamed. I could lose myself swinging for hours on end. Dad knows that, and I now have the most beautiful swing, with an inscription—"Built for Christal, My Little Girl." Each of his three children received a one-of-a-kind swing, made by the loving hands of our father for Christmas that year.

Shortcuts are not Dad's style, and of course, he went about the process of building our swings with the utmost care and attention to detail. His grandfather was a blacksmith and built chairs and rockers by hand; some are still in our family. Dad followed his pattern, cutting each board by hand and sanding off the edges before assembling our swings. Thirty hours of work put into each structure, tediously focusing on every portion, no time-saving alternative routes were taken—giving his best for his children.

We are all his favorite, and we know it; just as you are your Father's favorite. There is nothing He wouldn't do for you. Why? Because you are His special child created in His image by His loving hands. Isaiah 64:8 affirms this, "But now, O Lord, You are our Father; we are the clay, and You are our potter; and we all are the work of Your hand" (MEV). The Father fashioned and formed you perfectly in His image, no shortcuts, only the best plans for His children.

THREE BATTLESHIPS

Dad will say he's not much of a conversationalist, which is true; however, when he does decide to chime in, you should lean in and listen. He told me once of a struggling mother who felt her contribution to the Lord was minuscule. "I had so many aspirations and dreams for ministry, yet all I do is stay home and raise these five children," she told her small group. Sharing with Dad how I had, at times, felt that way when my children were young and the difficulties of keeping in perspective the beauty of the call of parenthood, I asked him how he responded. I will never forget his reply: "From a child on, I was told by others I would be a missionary, but never got in my little canoe and paddled upstream to do my own thing; I just stayed home and built three battleships."

His life's mission and calling were raising his three children. We were his fame, and along his journey of fatherhood, the knowledge that he was equipping and building the Kingdom through us never left the forefront of his mind. He knew his mission, his calling—his family—was his greatest achievement. I was reminded of Dad while reading the story of Cincinnatus, a private citizen who became a legend to the Romans because of his selfless leadership during times of war. On two occasions, he was given supreme power to lead his country, and as soon as he possibly could, surrendered his leadership to return to his family and farm. Fame and fortune were not his high calling, what he longed for, or where he found his contentment. In essence, he said, "No thanks, I will pass on accolades and success. Just give me my family and my farm."

Cincinnatus' story echo's my dad's mindset; execute what is expected, and come back to what is of true importance—family. Family is his mantra that continually plays in his heart and mind, and for those of us who are blessed to be included in that unit, we are fully aware of where we stand in his pecking order. Immersion into every part of our lives brings him the greatest joy and pride. Many promotions and advancements were afforded to him over the years; however, being pulled away from family was out of the question. What truly mattered in the long run gave way to the corporate ladder of success and opinions of man.

I am a Daddy's girl, and bragging on my dad comes quite easily. Maybe, I should tone it down, but I have been blessed with an amazing earthly father. I understand how rare that can be and what a wonderful gift I have been given. Throughout my life, I have seen the parallels of my dad and the heavenly Father time and time again. Lessons I have learned about the love, patience, and faithfulness of the Lord was taught by the example of my dad. There is nothing he cannot fix or create—he is never annoyed by me; he is a fabulous storyteller and writer; he loves God and His Word; family is a priority; he is strong, but gentle; I could go on and on. Sounds a lot like Jesus, doesn't it?

As the Father began speaking to me concerning this book, what I should write, and the correlation between Him and my dad, I experienced one of my most supernatural moments with Him. I search for the words to adequately describe the encounter as He took me back to my early childhood. Almost as if the Father allowed me to feel those precious moments once again, nestled in my father's strong arms, experiencing perfect peace, and receiving calm assurance of his love and acceptance.

I was back as that little girl, and the enemy's lies and incessant pounding on my thoughts came to a screeching halt—rest prevailed, and He held me. I could feel my dad's loving embrace, and all my worries melted away. I found myself at ease, in perfect peace, and enjoying that safe place where I could bare my soul. This place of rest is where trust thrives. Relaxing in His presence, we are assured He is well able to care for our every need, and peace overshadows doubts and fear. He's got us, not partially, but completely in every nook and cranny of our life. As He promised in Isaiah 26, when our minds focus on Him and His overwhelming love that goes beyond human understanding, we will never be forsaken.

APPENDIX 1

Finding Success

We were newlyweds. My wife, Sharon, was a youth pastor. My day job was counseling troubled adolescents, and my side gig was leading worship at our church. We were living the dream—fresh out of college, and we both had paying ministry jobs we enjoyed. And, as an unexpected bonus, we could pay the bills! We bought a little house. Once I adjusted to the low ceilings and figured out I needed to duck when I walked under the fan, all was well. That is, until the Lord pushed us out of our newly built nest.

The Lord was calling us to start a church. Church planting was in my long-term plans, but it was not in my immediate ones. I was twenty-two. Too young! Also, we'd be changing denominations, so support from a sending church wasn't in the cards. But, God said, "Go!" To make matters worse, He confirmed it pretty clearly.

It seemed we were going to move; however, I was terrified and needed some assurance. So, as always, I called Dad. In one sense, it's pointless to ask Dad for advice, because he never gives an answer. Many times I've sought Dad's input, knowing all along that an answer wouldn't be coming from him. He doesn't give answers; he asks questions. He wants us to get there on our own, and he trusts us to do the work. But I still call.

"Dad, I'm thinking of coming home and planting a church. What do you think?" I gave him the backstory and told him how I felt God was confirming it to Sharon and me. I was so scared! But if Dad agreed, I'd feel a lot more secure. This was a big one; maybe he'd cast a vote for once! Nope. Not even close. Instead, I got one of his patented replies: "Ask your other Dad."

He knew I'd already heard from a higher authority than himself, so there was no chance he was going to be my crutch. Dad understood that if he told me that he thought it was a great idea, then on the hard days (which he surely knew were coming), I could look back and wonder if I'd really heard from God or just felt confident because Dad was on board.

I already knew what I needed to do. I moved passed the fear, and it was time to pack. It was nice to have such a clear sense of calling. God had put us up to this, and that sounded like a pure adventure. That said, we knew enough about the Bible to understand that callings don't come with guarantees. I love Hebrews 11, the Hall of Faith! Who doesn't? But I can't shake those pesky verses at the end where the stories are recounted of those who obeyed God, and then they failed fantastically (and often fatally)—all while being obedient! Or what about all those prophets in the Old Testament? Isaiah's call was to spit in the wind (Isaiah 6:1-10). Every time Jeremiah did what he was told, he got beat up and thrown into a ditch (or so it seems). I found some comfort in God's propensity to bless the ignorant and ill-equipped, but I certainly didn't find comfort in my ineptitude.

I had recently attended a conference with a then largely unknown speaker, Erwin McManus. He spent the weekend talking about Jonathan and his young, unnamed armorbearer. McManus later wrote a book about this, *Chasing Daylight*. Jonathan's Dad (King Saul) was in hiding along with what was left of his pathetically tiny, under-resourced army. The Lord had promised victory, but Saul wasn't so sure anymore. McManus then shared how Jonathan and his armorbearer hatched a terrible plan—functionally a suicide mission—with no guarantee of success. God had promised victory to the Israelites, but He had not promised zero casualties. This was madness!

McManus continued by giving Jonathan's reason for pursuing their enemies. "'Let's go across to the outpost of those pagans,' Jonathan said to his armor bearer. 'Perhaps the LORD will help us, for nothing can hinder the LORD. He can win a battle whether he has many warriors or only a few!'" (1 Samuel 14:6 NLT). McManus responded, "PERHAPS! Perhaps, the Lord will help us! Let's go pick a fight with an entire army because MAYBE God will intervene!" McManus was shouting now. "Isn't that great!?"

It was great. My heart was racing. It was all I wanted. God's plan to save the world is the Church, and the gates of hell will not prevail against it! There are no guarantees of individual success when you give your life to serve the Church, unless, of course, obedience alone amounts to success. What if the only outcome that matters is trusting the Lord when He calls? The author of Hebrews sure seemed to think so.

Our little house sold quickly and at a profit. We had $14,000! This was an unimaginable fortune—$14,000! We moved into my grandma's basement. We had a microwave and a mini-fridge. We were set. CORRECTION: We had a microwave, a mini-fridge, and $14,000! The plan was simple: plant a church that could help support us before the money ran out.

We were in our twenties and practically invincible. Sleep was optional. Ramen noodles were a feast. We didn't care to work insane hours because we were doing it together! But, as it turns out, planting a church is really, really hard. After about a year, we realized that $14,000 wasn't an infinite fortune. It was dwindling. After two years, we were getting nervous. December 2006 was month 28 of the church plant. January would mark a new year and, for us, a new reality: the money would be gone.

But then, something unexpected happened. Our financial board met and decided that the church would be able to support us, beginning in January. We were ecstatic! Every prayer was answered, and every dream came true! It was down to the wire, but WE MADE IT!

While we were still celebrating God's faithfulness, another call came in. It was from a family friend. She had been praying for us and wanted to give us a financial gift. At the time, the maximum gift you could give someone without that person being taxed was $7,000 per calendar year. She had decided to give us $7,000 on December 31, and another $7,000 on January 1. Not only was the Church able to support us, but God gave us the $14,000 back! Our only prayer had been for the money to last. Neither of us had even considered that He might give it all back.

It might be tempting to conclude that was when we could declare "success." Not so. It was encouraging. It was a miracle. It was one marker based on an earthly measure. But for 28 months, we succeeded and failed hundreds of times, and we've done the same thousands of times since. We've seen lots of miracles. We've also had our teeth kicked in a few times (figuratively, at least) and wondered if we could get back up. We've wondered if we even should.

There were no guarantees of success when we started the church. There aren't any guarantees today, as we try to lead that church. Well, maybe there's one—the guarantee that trusting God is a success.

—Aaron McCarter, Lead Pastor
Vineyard Church, Maryville

APPENDIX 2

I Am His

Like my sister, Christal, I've always been a Daddy's girl. When I was born, my parents were expecting a boy. Surprise! Daddy always told me that he picked me up and said to my mom, "This one's mine." I had a head full of black hair and a crooked little nose from being in the same position for so long before I was born. Daddy held me all night while keeping my nose in the correct spot so I'd be ready for my newborn pictures the next morning. Many times, throughout my life, undoubtedly when I needed to hear it most, my daddy would remind me of this story and say, "You're mine." It has always grounded me and made me feel loved.

A few years ago, I was going through an extremely trying time. I had recently been part of a life group led by my father-in-law. It was about the Holy Spirit. We were challenged to say a very specific prayer every day: "Lord, show me; change me; fill me." I had prayed this prayer every day without fail, yet I felt little change. The group had been over for months, and I continued to pray the prayer. I knew there was something that was holding me back from what God intended for me, but I didn't know what. Through a series of events that were "brutiful" (brutal and beautiful), as my husband would say, God answered my prayer. At first, and for some time, I felt farther from God than I ever had. I was greatly humbled and broken, however, when He showed me that I had unforgiveness in my heart that I thought I had resolved. He removed it and truly changed me. He gave me a new heart and filled it with His love. During that time, He spoke to me through Scripture, other people, and sermons but, more than anything, He used the words of my daddy to help my roots grow deeper and to help me feel safe and loved. He daily told me, "You're mine."

Every time I see a willow tree, I think of my daddy. He has said many times that he loves them, and I'm sure that's why they're one of my favorite trees. About a month ago, for Mother's Day, my husband planted one for me in our field near our creek. I love it. Although the tree is still small, every time I'm on my deck, I look at it and imagine what it will be in time. I know that it will need to be watered and properly cared for as its roots are getting established. I wonder if Jeremiah was referring to a willow when writing these verses?

> But blessed are those who trust in the LORD and have made the LORD their hope and confidence. They are like trees planted along a riverbank, with roots that reach deep into the water. Such trees are not bothered by the heat or worried by long months of drought. Their leaves stay green, and they never stop producing fruit (Jeremiah 17:7-8 NLT).

During my time of pruning and change, I repeatedly referred to that verse, and this one written by Paul:

> When I think of all this, I fall to my knees and pray to the Father, the Creator of everything in heaven and on earth. I pray that from his glorious, unlimited resources he will empower you with inner strength through his Spirit. Then Christ will make his home in your hearts as you trust in him. Your roots will grow down into God's love and keep you strong. And may

Learning to Trust the Father's Heart

you have the power to understand, as all God's people should, how wide, how long, how high, and how deep his love is. May you experience the love of Christ, though it is too great to understand fully. Then you will be made complete with all the fullness of life and power that comes from God (Ephesians 3:14-19 NLT).

We went on vacation as a family every year. The summer I turned ten years old, we went to Sanibel Island in Florida. I have many fond memories from that trip: my new black bathing suit with hot pink hearts, renting a giant yellow water trike, the pure white sand, the crystal-clear water, and standing on our balcony seeing the endless ocean. While I may not remember every detail, the one experience I can still see vividly in my mind's eye is going to dig for sand dollars.

We had been playing at the water's edge for some time when my daddy started to go out farther. I wasn't much of a swimmer, so I didn't follow. After a little while, he motioned for my little brother, Aaron, and me to join him. He seemed so far away, but the water was below his waist. Although I was nervous, I started wading toward him. Aaron, who was a fantastic swimmer, got to him in no time at all. As I waded, the water became deeper and darker, and I could no longer see the sand under my feet. I stopped. My daddy encouraged me to come a little closer. I remember pouting because Aaron got there before I did. Why wasn't he scared? I continued slowly, taking tiny steps. I didn't even try to swim to them.

The water, once relatively still, was now around my chest and moving because of a passing boat. I stopped again. My daddy prodded for me to continue. Reluctantly, I inched my way closer, but as the water approached my neck, I froze. My daddy and little brother were close enough that I could hear their voices. They called for me to come to them. I wanted to, but I couldn't. The water was shallower where they were even though they were farther out than I was. As I stood there watching them, I noticed them reaching down into the water and then shooting up with something in their hands. Aaron was squealing with excitement, and his little hands were getting quite full. I desperately wanted to be with them, but I stood terrified with tears in my eyes. I couldn't go any farther.

Daddy noticed that I was scared, and he came closer to me. He stretched out his hand, which was only about ten feet away, and told me to swim to him. He assured me that I'd be able to stand without the water going over my head as soon as I reached him. Although I was still afraid, I believed him. I had swum to him many times before. He always kept me safe. I knew I could trust him, so I fought back the tears and swam as he cheered me on. In only a few seconds, I had hold of my daddy's hand, and he was pulling me to the shallow waters. Soon I was collecting sand dollars too. We made a beautiful memory, and I learned a lifelong lesson about trust.

Isn't that just like our God? He goes before us, but He is never far from our reach. We're being stretched as we learn to step out in faith, with His encouragement all along the way. What He has waiting for us is an adventure that we don't want to miss.

I've learned to trust my heavenly Father just as I trust my earthly father. I've never once questioned whether my daddy would take care of me or be there instantly if I needed him, and the same is true for my heavenly Father. In the fall of 2017, God directed my attention to Isaiah 43:1-7 (NLT). He told me to replace the names Jacob and Israel with the names of my husband, children, and me.

But now, O [Nick, Farah, Elysia, and Egan], listen to the LORD who created you. O [Nick, Farah, Elysia, and Egan] . . . Do not be afraid, for I have ransomed you. I have called you by name; you are mine. When you go through deep waters [and great troubles], I will be with you. When you go through rivers of difficulty, you will not drown. When you walk through the fire of oppression, you will not be burned up; the flames will not consume you. For I am the LORD, your God, the Holy One of Israel, your Savior. I gave Egypt as a ransom for your freedom; I gave Ethiopia and Seba in your place. Others [died that you might live]. I traded their lives for yours because you are precious to me. You are honored, and I love you. Do not be afraid, for I am with you. I will gather you and your children from east and west. I will say to the north and south, "Bring my sons and daughters back to Israel from the distant corners of the earth. Bring all who claim me as their God, for I have made them for my glory. It was I who created them."

As a Christian, my roots must continue to grow deeply in Him every day of my life. I must never stop producing the good fruit that develops as a result of God's love in me. I am His. I will not be afraid. He will be with me through times of difficulty when the water gets too deep. Although I will walk through the fire, He won't allow the flames to consume me. He has called me by name, and I am precious to Him. Just as I am my daddy's, I am His.

—Farah Rains
Children's Director
Canvas Church